With my
Love, Ang Psalm

Life
Interrupted

Angel Renee Hovey

PublishAmerica
Baltimore

This book is dedicated to you, Gracie.
I love you always and forever.

Chapter One

The Naked Truth

What is it that we think we know about abortion? We may know the procedures in which they use to perform abortions. We may know that it was legalized by Roe VS Wade in the 70's. We may know that it is wrong depending on our background and upbringing. We may know where the closest abortion clinic is and may have even protested there. We may know which politicians support abortion and which ones don't, but is that it? Have we looked any deeper into the truth of it? Do any of us really know who's having abortions? Are we reaching out to them only before they make this choice and then condemning them after or are we still there as believers? Are we still there ready to help them heal from an emotional bondage they had no idea they were walking into?

So let us ask ourselves the bigger question; the only question that should matter right now. Who are these young women and how can we really make a difference? You might ask yourself why this question is the only one that matters. The answer is very simple and very straight forward. If we know who they are, and if we know where they are, then we have the root to the tree of prevention. If we can prevent a large majority of abortions, we can not only save the lives of both the unborn and their parents, but we can change the face of legalized abortion in this country.

Are you thinking that you already know who? You might assume as most do these are young women who come from broken homes, who have been raped or abused. Women who use abortion as a method of birth control and who haven't been taught right from wrong. Women who can't afford more children or come from poverty stricken areas. If you believe these types of women are those having abortions, you are right. There is only one problem...**they are the minority!**

I hope you are wondering who then the majority is. Are you ready for the answer? You might be startled, or will you? The answer is there, you know it, and you just don't want to face it. You don't want to face it because it is the naked and ugly truth! It is this truth that tells us that **our** children, **our** daughters, **our** sons are leading the statistics in abortions! How can this be? We have raised them up in church! We have taught them right from wrong and we have watched them go through the stages of salvation and baptism. Not my daughter, not my son, not in my family! My children would never do this!

I must tell you that you are not alone if this is how you feel. Most parents, especially those proclaiming to be believers, feel this way for a couple of reasons. First, because they want to believe in, trust and protect their children. Second, as a parent there isn't one of us who wants to feel as if we have somehow failed our children in the worst of ways. Where did we go wrong? How did we not see this? How could we have prevented this? These are a few of the various questions you might ask yourself for the rest of your lives if you had to face this situation.

We all want to believe that our children will always make the right choices and if they make some mistakes abortion most certainly won't be one of them. Please remember this; every situation is different. What we must accept is that we are not perfect therefore we cannot be perfect parents. We also must conclude that we can only do our best in raising them and realize that they have a personal accountability for their own actions. They solely dominate their own ability to control the choices they do make. Yes, we have the power as a parent to influence those choices and must take this as seriously as life and death; however, the end result of any choice is ultimately theirs. If you have or will experience abortion in your family, beating yourself up as a parent isn't going to help anyone. That is why learning what you can do now is vital to saving your children and possibly your grandchildren.

Let's be certain we understand that this is not a condemnation of Christian parents. It is a cry for **Believer's** of all ages to build a barrier against Satan's lies. It is a plea for us to come to the understanding of who Satan is and how he will use delicate and emotional situations to control our children and the choices they make. He is using our beliefs, our morals, our values and our relationships with our children against us! He is doing it and in some cases, he is winning the battle.

The good news is there are two sides to this naked truth. The good? *There is hope.* That hope is that we are assured through scripture that Satan may win some battles, but he will not win the war! Holding up signs against abortion at the clinics or lined down the street is one avenue of letting others know where you stand. In itself, many women have been saved from the clutches of abortion including Norma McCorvey, better known as Jane Roe of Roe vs. Wade. Obviously we are reaching people through this means so please continue, just do it with love and compassion. These women are already vulnerable to judgment. You will never reach them without careful and sincere affection for their situation. Pray that God will guide you and lead you in all you say and do.

In turn, there is a problem greater than the agony of organizing and gathering volunteers to protest abortion. The problem is according to the numbers, we don't need to go to the abortion clinics to save babies; we need to start within our homes and churches! The welcomed news is that there are four basic steps we can follow as parents. These steps have the capability of transforming not only our own lives in our walk with God but in transforming the lives of our children in the choices they make. As we journey through this book together, ask God to prepare your heart in accepting the truth of abortion. Ask Him to open the door of the understanding that we have a great responsibility to be aware of the possibility of abortion within our own homes. If you are uncertain or question the validity of what I have already shared, you better keep reading. You won't believe it!

Statistics Breakdown

These statistics are taken from the Guttmacher Institute; it is a secular foundation but has the most accurate statistics concerning abortion or any sexual and reproductive health issue worldwide. I have also pulled statistics from Faith based information sites which reflect the same results. If you would like to research these statistics you can find information on websites, crisis centers and different programs affiliated with abortion in the back of this book. Only a number of them were used as resources for this project. I felt it necessary to provide each reader with as much information as possible to use at your own disposal.

Source: Guttmacher Institute, Facts on induced abortion in the United States, *In Brief,* New York: Guttmacher Institute, 2008, <http://www.guttmacher.org/pubs/fb_induced_abortion.pdf>, accessed DATE.

Basic Information on those obtaining abortions in America:

- Nearly half of all pregnancies among American women are unintended and *4 IN 10 are terminated by abortion.*
- 22% of all pregnancies (excluding miscarriages) end in abortion
- In 2005, 1.2 million abortions were performed
- From 1973 through 2005, more than 45 million legal abortions occurred
- *At least half of American women will experience an unintended pregnancy* by *age 45 and at current rates; about one-third will have had an abortion.*

Who Has Abortions
* **50% of US women obtaining abortions are younger than 25**
* Women ages 20-24 obtain 33% of all abortions
* *43% of women obtaining abortions identify themselves as Protestant*
* 27% of women obtaining abortions identify themselves as Catholic
* Women who have never been married obtain two-thirds of all abortions
* About 60% of abortions are obtained by

women who have one or more children

There it is the naked truth of abortion. Why do I refer to it as the naked truth? It is abortion without bias, without secrecy, without argument. It is fact and we can't ignore it, we can't run away from it, we have to face it. We have to face the reality that almost half of all abortions in this country are obtained by young women who claim to be believers. They are women from our churches, our schools, our communities and may even be in our own homes.

Let's take a closer look at the breakdown of the numbers of abortions obtained by women under the age of 25. This is significant because there is only a short window of opportunity for parents, grandparents, teachers, pastors or any adult to advocate abstinence and abortion prevention. That window is between the ages of 12 and 16. This is of my own opinion and I came to this conclusion based on what I believe to be the biblical age of accountability, which is twelve, and the average age of the onset of sexual activity, which is sixteen. In all cases, this is dependent on the maturity of the individual child.

For those parents who do talk about sex with their children, we usually don't start that process before the age of 12. By the time our children are able to drive a motor vehicle, they have found some independence as well as a private place to spend time with someone they care for in a romantic way. As they are coming into their teen years they are still talking to us, asking questions, searching for the answers. If we aren't furnishing those answers in a real and godly way when they are willing to hear us, someone else is going to do it for us. I can almost guarantee you someone else's answers won't be the same as yours. How important is it? Just keep reading.

—If 1,200,000 (1.2 million) babies were aborted last year that means that 516,000 (43%) babies were aborted by those proclaiming to be believers.

—If 516,000 babies were aborted by proclaimed believers then 258,000 (50%) babies were aborted by proclaimed believers under the age of 25.

Do you realize what you just read? Is it sinking in yet? 516,000 babies were lost to young women who tell people they are a Christian. Many of them probably get up on Sunday go to church, maybe sing in the choir, help teach a class and spend their summers as counselors at church camp. They are pretending; they are trying to forget about their choice, they are trying desperately to keep their deepest, darkest secret hidden from the only world they know. Why? They fear judgment, they fear a lack of forgiveness, and they fear abandonment.

Why then did they make this choice? The very same reasons you just read. It is these lies of Satan that encouraged them to have sex in the first place. It is the same lies he uses each time. They produce such powerful feelings that he can use them to motivate sex, and when sex produces pregnancy he uses them to motivate abortion. Satan is the tempter, not God. Satan knows us much better than we can fathom. He knows how to stir our desires and he most certainly knows how to stir the desires of our children.

"When tempted, no one should say, "God is tempting me." For God cannot be tempted by evil, nor does he tempt anyone; but each one is tempted when, by his own evil desire, he is dragged away and enticed. Then after desire has conceived, it gives birth to sin; and sin, when it is full grown, gives birth to death." James 1:13-15

Is this not the exact description of abortion? The desire for a girl becomes a live temptation and entices her; the conception of the sin. She gives into it and becomes sexually active. You could say this is the giving birth of the sin. She then finds herself pregnant; the sin is now full grown. What happens next? Abortion seems to be the only option to finding freedom from the situation, it is the bringing forth of death.

Understand that I use the "girl" in the example only due to the fact that it is her body that ultimately withstands the abortion process. I am in no way removing any young man from the circumstance or responsibility that he should equally share.

So what goes through the minds of these young people? What reasons do they give for choosing such a desperate option? Through my own personal research as well as information gathered through other researchers the following are the most frequently stated reasons for abortion given by those who were raised in a faith based or Christian lifestyle.

10 Reasons why young women chose to have abortions.

1. I can't let my parents know
2. I can't support myself or a baby, I want to finish school
3. It is legal
4. My boyfriend will break up with me if I don't have an abortion.

5. My mother is pressuring me to have an abortion

6. Getting pregnant was an accident; I just want to undo it

7. I don't like what pregnancy will do to my body

8. It's not really a baby, it just a blob of tissue

9. I'm pregnant because I was raped

10. I have to have an abortion, there is no other way

Let's go back to those few things we may know about this issue. We may know about the procedures but are we aware of the danger those procedures can cause the mother? Have we ever thought about that as a tool to fuel our fight against abortion? We may know that it was legal in the 70's but do we know who Roe VS Wade is? Did you know that the 'Jane Roe' in this fight was never even able to obtain an abortion due to the length of the trial? Did you also know that after years of misery working in support of her win, she was reached by a minister protesting outside the clinic in which she worked? He didn't bombard her with signs or by yelling chants; he simply talked to her when she took a smoke break. He reached her through love. Did you know that she is now one of the main stream leaders in the fight against legalized abortion?

What are we, as believers, doing to assist in the fight against abortion? Are we chanting words outside a clinic while we hold up a sign that says "MURDERER!" Do we really think we are going to reach anyone that way? Are we laying down our judgment on those we know who have made this choice in their past so that they may never feel they can find forgiveness from a Savior if they can't find forgiveness from His people? Are we simply complaining and condemning while we stand outside the church sanctuary? Or are we are ready to stand up and change history? Are you ready to do whatever it takes to save even one unborn child? Are you ready to do whatever it takes to save even one lost and broken soul? I am and I hope that you will stand with me.

Chapter Two

Why?

Now that we have established who is having abortions, it is important for us to try to comprehend the why's in the minds of these women. It seems impossible to actually come up with a valid reason that would justify such an act as this. *This is where understanding comes in.* At the time of choice their mind is under the influence of Satan. As Christians, we are all very aware that if we are not of God, we are of the devil. What am I trying to say here? If they were not right with God, they were living in sin. When you are living in sin you have no true clarity of consequence. These women were twisting and mutilating justification until it fit into a rationalized theory of having to abort their babies.

Whatever their reason, it was the only way they felt they could deal with their situation. At the point where you feel that you have justified the choice to abort, you also believe you have no other options. They see the pregnancy as the absolute worst situation they could face. Satan begins to whisper these lies in their very fragile minds.

—There is no forgiveness for what I have done.

—My family won't love me anymore!

—People will see me as an outcast and I won't be able to work in the church.

—God can never love me again so why does it matter what I do now.

—Abortion can't be as bad as everyone thinks; it's legal.

—I have already screwed up so much my family would never be able to forgive me for this, I have no other choice.

These are just a few of the thoughts that go through the minds of these young ladies. With each thought there is enormous emotional and mental torment. It is this torment that Satan feeds on and it is this torment these women allow to control them. You see, they are no longer logical or sensible; they are lost in every sense of the word. In most cases all they are hearing is whatever Satan is whispering to them. If they have found someone that they can confide in it usually isn't someone that they associate with church because it is not safe. Safety at this point for these women is in those who are usually lost as well, those who will not judge them for their choice.

So, if this is how it happens, what can we do or how will we know they are in trouble? In most cases you won't; it is that simple. That is why you need to prepare them before this point comes to pass. Let's say that you didn't follow every step of this book but you did take the advice on talking with your child about abortion. Your daughter writes to you, because she can't face you, and tells you she is pregnant, scared and so very sorry. She chooses life and finds her way through it with you by her side. Ten years later you ask her if she had ever thought about having an abortion. Her reply is that she thought about it but would never go through with it because of that one conversation you once had with her. She tells you she was scared and unsure of your reaction but she could remember you conveying that if she ever became pregnant you never wanted her to choose abortion. She remembered how you told her that you would be hurt and disappointed but you would be there for her. So she chose life because you chose to talk about it.

It happens, more than you can conceive, it happens to our kids, our friends, our family members. I remember as I started this process and began to interview some of these women, the majority of those I spoke with were middle aged then but very young when they obtained their abortion. Others were still in their early and middle twenties, and some older. I was amazed at the revelation that age did not seem to matter. Some of these women had more than one abortion, can you imagine? Falling into the same lie over and over again? Have you ever done that? I think we all have at some point in our life because we are human. Still, the emotional and mental bondage of taking the life of their unborn whether it was once or four times cripples each of them in such a way that normalcy becomes misery and depression.

As you read the stories of these three women, I pray that you will try to put yourself in the very place they were at the time of their choice. Think about your family, your church, your parents, your friends. Really pause and ask yourself if you would have possibly considered it. It is easy to say that you would never do this until your there. The object here is to bring forth the realization that we cannot reach out to these women unless we feel a genuine compassion for their situation. I am not saying empathize with abortion, I am saying have compassion for where they were, where many of our girls are right now.

The identities of these women are confidential. We are all victims of Satan's lies. We have all failed God in some form and in most cases we all keep the worst of our sins to ourselves. These women have come forward to share their stories. They share their stories with the great hope that other young women can be saved.

Each of these women are beautiful. They have been through a great deal in their battle with abortion. They have given me permission to share their stories some written by their own hand and some written by mine. I have taken the information from the interview process and now share their stories with you.

Twice Redeemed

Young and beautiful, she was the pinnacle of what a young Christian lady should be. Other members of the church youth group looked up to her and trusted her. Her voice was soft and her spirit was sweet. As she grew older she became interested in many things including a young man. This young man was handsome and charming and their relationship began to blossom. As their dating progressed the physical relationship between the two of them was following suit until it evolved into sexual activity. The news came hard for both of them; she was pregnant. They were so young and they weren't ready for this. They weren't ready for the responsibility, nor were they sure they were meant for each other. She could not control her fear. Fear of the church excluding her, shunning her and condemning her. Fear of the other members of her youth group that looked up to her. What would they think? Would they ever speak to me again? The torment and shame of what she had done became too much to bear. She and the father decided abortion was their only alternative. Distraught, she made herself go; reminding herself this was the only option she had. Twenty five years later, she is married to that young man but nothing seems right. She has asked for forgiveness and lived with the torment and anguish of the choice she made so long ago. I can't find happiness, she says to herself over and over again. She now has three beautiful children and there is still a part of her that can't find peace. She has no idea how to love herself or find herself *worthy of love from God or people. She deals with this everyday until finally she hears God's calling upon her life. Broken, she runs to him, she cries out to a God who truly loves her and begs for his forgiveness. As time passes she knows that God's grace has showered her and his forgiveness of her choice has given her a freedom that she can not describe. Her children are now young adult as she feels the leading of God to share her abortion experience with her only daughter. She struggles and fights this request from God she begins to believe the twisted words Satan whispers in her ear once again. She can not tell her daughter, what would her beautiful little girl think of her. She would never look at her the same again. Torn and emotionally fragile, she chooses not to share this choice of her past with her daughter. After all the suffering she has faced, the pain of abortion comes once again into her life. Just months after she made the decision to discard God's leading in sharing her abortion, the news comes and is far more difficult to bear than she could have ever imagined. Her beautiful little girl now must deal with the agony of her own abortion experience. In despair she cries out, how did this happen? Why didn't I listen, why didn't I tell her? Why didn't I realize that God was trying to help me save my grandchild? She makes herself and*

God a promise...this is a mistake I will not make again.

This wonderful and amazing woman has kept her promise. She has since played a leading role in reaching many women who have made this same devastating decision through an abortion recovery program, including her daughter. She has allowed God to use her story to bring forth healing and the understanding of forgiveness.

Lost in Despair

In the midst of ending an abusive and destructive marriage I found myself falling in love with another man who was married. After a short affair beginning in June and lasting only three months, I had moved to Texas for job training when I found out I was pregnant. Knowing the father of my child was married to someone else and out of my life, this left me with few options. I had no home, couldn't drive and no where to turn. Seeking advice from anyone, I realized how very alone I was. To my surprise the father of the baby showed up looking for me. After sharing the news with him about my condition, he also was shocked and confused. He made it very clear to me at that time that any decision was mine to make and mine alone. Lost in despair, I reluctantly made the choice to abort. I can't explain the horrible torment of the procedure itself. It felt as if someone was ripping my insides out. That night all I could do was cry. I wanted to end my own life because I felt I didn't deserve to live. Later, the father knocked on my door and when I told him what I had done, he was so angry and hurt. I heard him weeping in the other room and it just added to the anguish and shame that I was already facing. I found myself furious with him as I believed he wanted no part of a relationship with me or the baby. It is 25 years later and he and I have just ended our 23 year marriage. We have two sons that are the joy of our lives but the pain from that one day in August of 1979 will never leave us. We still can't talk about it because I just fall apart, I can't handle it. If there is anything that I can say to someone contemplating abortion it is this; DON'T DO IT! You may never recover."

Judgment Strikes Back!

I grew up in a Christian home, came from a family that was respected. I attended a Christian school and thought that I had this 'living my life right' thing all figured out. I remember my junior year in high school my English teacher gave us an assignment of a term paper. She also informed us that we could add our own work to it if we saw fit and it tied into the project. I chose to do my term paper on abortion. I hated the idea of it and I hated the people who chose it. I couldn't understand why anyone would choose to kill their own baby. I finished my paper and added to the end of it a poem. This poem made a great impact on my teacher, my family, my church and my friends. At one point it was considered for a plastic card printing to be handed out at the abortion clinics. The poem was called "MOMMY WHY?"

Mommy Why

Mommy, Daddy are you there?
I know I'm only tiny but I'm living right in here.
Now I can see my hands, my feet and little toes,
I wish that I could show you how much I'm starting to grow.
Everyday I'm getting bigger and new things I can see
I know when you are hurting and it really bothers me.
Lately you've been testy and I can't understand why,
I wish that I could help you so that you would never cry.
Mommy, I'm so excited, only a few more months to

go,

I hope you name me Holly and together we can grow.

Mommy! Mommy Wait! What is happening to me?

Something's really hurting, I'm scared—I'm sacred to look and see!

It keeps on getting closer and I can't seem to get away!

Mommy, Why won't you help me? Mommy! Mommy Wait!

Now it's taken my arms, my little legs and feet

It's getting very dark and I'm very, very weak.

I guess I'll never know why didn't really care

But mommy for a while, I lived in you somewhere.

I guess I'll never see you or get to have you hold me tight

But I wish someday you could tell me why you didn't help me fight.

I remember writing this poem. Every time I read or see it, I feel sick. I recall watching The Silent Scream movie for this report and I hated what I saw. I said that I would never make this choice and I hated those who did. After graduating high school, I went on to receive my license in cosmetology and followed that with going off to a Christian college. Before the end of my first year of college I was asked to leave due to becoming sexually active. I will never forget the hurt and shame that I caused my family. The church we attended at the time was outwardly disgusted with me as well. I was running and ran right into the arms of my first husband. We married when I was just 20 years old. We had our first child within the same year and were divorced by the time our son was just 4 months old. I don't know how I got so lost but I did. By the following year I found out that I was pregnant again, unsure of the father and already a single mother. The only thing that went through my mind was that I couldn't let this happen. My family was already so disappointed and this would only ensure their perception of my many failures. I went back and forth so many times until I finally came up with a great lie to tell my best friend so she would go with me to the abortion clinic. It was the only choice I had, that is what I believed. I didn't even know how far along I was until I got there. I found out that I was in my twelfth week. I remember lying on that table and crying. I was so afraid of everything. I started to try to get up; I didn't want to do this. I gave in and laid there never to be the same again. The white line painted on the pavement of the road that led home that day became my companion as thoughts of my baby ran

*through my head. I couldn't believe what I had done.
It is by far, the greatest tragedy of my life.*

These stories are just a few of those shared with me in the research for this project. With each one I cried. With each one I felt their pain, their fear and the shame they carried so visibly on their shoulders. With each one, I realized that it was their fear that made them weak. It was their fear that drove them to believe they had no other way out. I realized that Satan smiled because he knew he had them, he knew how to get them. He used the thing that meant the most to them, their loved ones.

I wonder at this moment as you read this how you are reacting right now. Are you wiping away the tears from your eyes as you sense the torment of these women? Do you understand how powerful we are in the lives of those we cherish? So powerful in fact, that our love and acceptance of them can be misconstrued into such a situation as this. May God help each of us see this world for what it really is, Satan's domain. May God help us reach out to those who need him no matter what they have done in their past. It is the soul of a man that God desires and it is that soul that only God can change.

You see, the Father does his work through his people and we must be willing to allow it. We must put aside our bias, our hatred, our racism, our pride and our judgment for God to have the opportunity to change the lives of people. And when God has this opportunity we begin to see the changes within our homes, our churches and our communities. It is only then that we can change the face of such a tragedy as abortion.

Chapter Three

What Does God Say?

It is unfortunate that the scriptures have been scrutinized in such a way that there has been a great misconception of God's view on the subject of abortion. There are many who believe that there are specific scriptures that show God's approval for the choice of abortion. These individuals have intertwined their own opinions and have confused the written and inspired word with the acceptance of today's lifestyles.

The truth lies not only in scripture but in the history of the time frame in which it was written. The scripture that is the heart of this controversy is Exodus 21:22-23. *"If men who are fighting hit a pregnant woman and she gives birth prematurely but there is no serious injury, the offender must be fined whatever the woman's husband demands and the court allows. But if there is serious injury, you are to take life for life, eye for eye, tooth for tooth, hand for hand, foot for foot, burn for burn, wound for wound, bruise for bruise."*

Some contend that this means that if a pregnant woman is injured, the assailant receives punishment in the same manner with which he injured the pregnant woman. However, if the woman miscarries, the assailant only pays a fine. They believe that the fetus, as they put it, is not viewed in the same manner as the woman. They believe that if the fetus were considered human the punishment for injuring the fetus would be the same punishment as that for injuring the pregnant woman.

Now, let's really look at this. First, if God did not care about the fetus, using the same terms as those who believe the above viewpoint, why would it even be mentioned that the woman was pregnant? Would this not be the case for any woman even if she weren't with child? Do woman who are not with child have no rights? Second, if we look again at the scripture it states, *"If men who are fighting hit a pregnant woman and she gives birth prematurely but there is no serious injury, the offender must be fined whatever the woman's husband and the courts allow."* It seems clear to me that God is talking about the child here. *"...she gives birth prematurely but there is no serious injury..."* Injury to the mother? No, I believe it refers to any injury to the child.

We know that God is a God of few words. The entire Bible that I read from is 1048 pages. I could not write about my entire life experiences in only 1048 pages. My point? God does not add something that does not need to be there. He speaks of a pregnant woman because he loves the child within the womb as well as the woman who carries that child.

Let me now refer back to the history of the time in which this particular scripture was written. We must consider the time frame if we are to have a clear understanding of any of the scriptures. Think about a movie you have seen or a book you have read. If it set in the 1800's could you really grasp the story if they were talking through text messages or wearing the clothes we see on the racks today? No, that is why movie directors and writers go out of their way to give a clear description of speech, setting, and way of life for the time frame they are focusing on. We must do the same so let's take a good look at it.

Most of us are familiar with the story of Abraham and Sarah. She desperately wanted to give her husband a child. So much so that she gave him one of her servants to bear a child for him. Imagine this for a moment. Would you allow your husband to lay with another woman and have his child? NO WAY! In today's society, we adopt, use fertility or simply accept that we will never bear children. During that period, it was simply unacceptable.

There are several accounts of situations similar to Sarah's throughout the Old Testament, but why? During this time, a child was seen as a blessing from God. The more children you had, the more God's hand was upon you. Women had several children and did not stop until they could physically not bear anymore offspring.

In the story of Jacob, Leah and Rachel, the sisters were practically racing to see who could give Jacob the most children. Genesis 30:1-3 *"When Rachel saw that she was not bearing Jacob any children, she became jealous of her sister. So she said to Jacob, "Give me children, or I'll die!" Jacob became angry with her and said, "Am I in the place of God, who has kept you from having children?" Then she said, "Here is Bilhah, my maidservant. Sleep with her so that she can bear children for me and that through her I too can build a family."* You can read on in the passages that follow to discover how Rachel and Leah continued this battle and how Jacob became the father of great numbers of children because of it. Do you see it? Such a desire of the women of that time to bear children? It was the pride of women and their husbands. It was the reality of God's blessing upon their life. When you take this factor into consideration you may now be able to understand that the reference to the pregnant woman had everything to do with the child she was carrying.

We must not allow Satan to antagonize us with the logic of others who are blind to the Word of God even when they read it. The truth can only be revealed through the scriptures when God is directing the understanding of the book that he has given us. Who better to ask what it means than the author himself?

I hope that you have a clearer view of God's position on abortion. If you do you may be asking, how then can we forgive those who have taken the life that God intended to be lived? The answer is again found in the scripture. II Chronicles 7:14 *"If my people, who are called by my name, will humble themselves and pray and seek my face and turn from their wicked ways, then I will hear from heaven and will forgive their sin and heal their land."* We forgive because he does.

One of the greatest stories in the Bible is about the woman who was brought to Jesus by the Pharisees as she was caught in midst of adultery. The Law of Moses was to stone any woman who did such an act as this but Jesus, in a carefree manner, began to simply write in the sand as the situation unfolded. *John 8:3-11"The teachers of the law and the Pharisees brought in a woman caught in adultery. They made her stand before the group and said to Jesus "Teacher, this woman was caught in the act of adultery. In the Law Moses commanded us to stone such women. Now what do you say?" They were using this question as a trap, in order to have a basis for accusing him. But Jesus bent down and started to write on the ground with his finger. When they kept on questioning him, he straightened up and said to them, "If any of you is without sin, let him be the first to throw a stone at her." "Again, he stooped down and wrote on the ground. At this, those who heard began to go away one at a time, the older ones first, until only Jesus was left, with the woman still standing there. Jesus straightened up and asked her, "Woman, where are they? Has no one condemned you?" "No one sir, she said." "Then neither do I condemn you" Jesus declared. Go now and leave your life of sin."*

This is the attitude and heart with which we are to love and forgive others. This is the example we are to follow. *Every* soul is to be saved! This is the desire of God's heart and the desire he has for our hearts.

David understood that God's forgiveness and love was much more than amazing, much greater than the universe and much stronger than the forces of many armies. After many failures in his walk with God, including the adultery with Bathseeba and the murder of her husband Uriah, David is still known as the man after God's own heart. If God had not given him forgiveness, or granted him a pardon or had not loved him even in the face of failure, we would not have the Bible as we know it today. David says it best in *Psalm 86:13.* *"For great is your love toward me; you have delivered me from the depths of the grave."*

I believe David also answers any lingering questions as to God's position on abortion in one of his greatest Psalms ever written, Psalm 139:1-18

"O Lord, you have searched me and you know me. You know when I sit and when I rise; you perceive my

thoughts from afar. You discern my going out and my lying down; you are familiar with all my ways. Before a word is on my tongue you know it completely, O Lord. You hem me in—behind and before; you have laid your hand upon me. Such knowledge is too wonderful for me, too lofty for me to attain. Where can I go from your Spirit? Where can I flee from your presence? If go up to the heavens, you are there; If I make my bed in the depths, you are there. If I rise on the wings of the dawn, if I settle on the far side of the sea, even there your hand will guide me, your right hand will hold me fast. I say, "Surely the darkness will hide me and the light become night around me." Even the darkness will not be dark to you; the night will shine like the day, for darkness is as light to you. **For you created my inmost being; you knit me together in my mother's womb. I praise you because I am fearfully and wonderfully made;** *your works are wonderful, I know that full well.* **My frame was not hidden from you when I was made in the secret place. When I was woven together in the depths of the earth, your eyes saw my unformed body, all the days ordained for me were written in your book before one of them came to be.** *How precious to me are your thoughts, O God! How vast is the sum of them! Were*

I to count them, they would outnumber the grains of sand. When I awake, I am still with you."

Chapter Four

Forgiving the Unforgivable

Forgiveness— to cease to feel resentment against.

To grant pardon for or remission of.

This chapter is going to require each of us to stop, really focus on God, and pray for him to guide every thought and feeling we have. To awaken within each of us what it is that we need to face about ourselves and what we need to do to change it. This chapter isn't just about forgiving others. It can relate to any feeling, thought or action against someone or against ourselves. Without God's forgiveness of our own personal sins, we would not have the opportunity of salvation. In the same way, without forgiving others, we also would not have the opportunity of salvation. ***Matthew 6:14 "For if you*** *forgive men when they sin against you, your heavenly Father will also forgive you. But if you do not forgive men their sins, your Father will not forgive your sins."*

For many of us this is a struggle. I am currently praying hard about forgiving someone that has been cruel and unkind to me. Unfortunately, I haven't always responded in the proper manner or in a way that would be most pleasing to God. I have had to ask for a lot of forgiveness over this. Can I really and truly forgive this person?

We all say that we can or have forgiven someone, it may even seem that way when we are around them but have we truly let it go? Here are a few things that will help you know for sure.

You haven't forgiven them if:
1. You avoid gatherings of every sort just to dodge them.
2. Even though you are smiling when they are talking to you, you still believe they are behind whatever the situation was that went badly.
3. You allow what they say and do to have an effect on your behavior.
4. You secretly wish for their failures to be

apparent to others.

If only one of these apply to how we feel, we are guilty of being unforgiving. If we can't forgive those who have wronged us, why would we still expect that God hears ours cries for redemption? Is there someone in your church, your family, your school, or your neighborhood that you are struggling to forgive? Do you know something that someone did and you just can't get past it?

The likelihood is that you can't get past it because you can't understand their situation. You probably never will, so you just have to get over it. I know...such a simple answer to a much larger problem. I believe there is no problem larger than its solution. What I have experienced with God is that his answers are always much simpler than I want them to be. I am usually so frustrated that I don't want to just get over it and let it go. I want God to come down from Heaven, part the red sea and show my assailant all their faults. In reality, God usually shows me mine. It is a most humbling experience.

The fact is that we can't control other people and their emotions, actions, or their state of mind. This is why it is pointless to be angry and bitter. Because it is how they control us. Does it seem that we become the angriest with our children or those who are closest to us? But in turn, those closest to us are the easiest to forgive. Why? Because we love them! It is easy to follow God's commands to forgive others when we love them. It is easy to forgive those who we know love us in return. As believers we are too truly forgive anyone, no matter what the situation. If we can do this with those we do not hold dear, we are showing the true heart of our Savior.

Jesus shared this same opinion in *Matthew 5:43-48. "You have heard that it was said, 'Love your neighbor and hate your enemy.' But I tell you: Love your enemies and pray for those who persecute you, that you may be sons of your Father in heaven. He causes his sun to rise on the evil and the good, and sends rain on the righteous and the unrighteous. If you love those who love you, what reward will you get? Are not even the tax collectors doing that? And if you greet only your brothers, what are you doing more than others? Do not even pagans do that? Be perfect, therefore, as your heavenly Father is perfect."*

The greatest test we can endure is to love our enemies. We sometimes dislike people because our personalities clash or we can find nothing in common to agree on. What if we are in a situation where an individual does some horrible act to our spouse or our children? How would we ever be able to forgive them? To forgive murderers, molesters, abusers, liars, cheaters; how do we do this? What I felt God was telling me was very simple. Be like Christ! He took on the sin of the world. Every horrible act, he bore, he suffered and he did it with great love. He allowed those who did these things to beat him, to mock him and to hang him on a cross. Then, he asked his Father to forgive them and he gave his life for that forgiveness. The only way we can ever love like Christ is to ask for the capability to do so.

We are humanly incapable of loving this way because we are born into sin. It is easy for us to love our children because we have a history with them, because they love us back. Just this morning, I was at my daughter's school watching her and her classmates give their oral reports on a famous character. Each student had to dress as their character which made it all the more interesting. I noticed that with each student their parent would raise a camera or camcorder to ensure they didn't miss anything. You knew which child belonged to which parent just by the ups and downs of the cameras. My point? A perfect example of how we are interested in only our own lives and the lives of those we love, those who love us. Would we take the time to video someone we didn't know, didn't love that wouldn't appreciate it? No, because that is our human nature.

Jesus was not of this world. Although he was born into sin, he carried a wisdom and understanding that we can never have on our own. He is able to see the needs of others, by the manner of their walk, the expression on their face and the look in their eye. He sees them; he sees the part we don't. So how do we love these people, especially our enemies if we are humanly incapable? We don't, we let God love them through us. We are incapable of healing the blind or moving a mountain, but Jesus says that we can do all things through him. Through him he tells that all things are possible. (Philippians 4:13) This means that if we break the barriers of our mind, give God complete control over us, then he can move a mountain through us. Only then can he heal the sick through us. It is about faith, about freedom, and about giving our entire being to God.

Let's take a look at Stephen, a man of God, one of my favorite men in the Bible. There are only seven accounts found in Acts that speak of Stephen. They are found in chapter 6:5-15, chapter 7:1, 54-55, 59, chapter 8:11, chapter 11:19, chapter 22:20. Only two of these scriptures refer to his ministry. The others give reference to the leading up to and actual events of his death. The two verses which speak of his ministry both state that **he was a man full of faith and power**. I would think that God was trying to make a point here, don't you? Both verses, both state the same thing in the same book in the same chapter. We usually only repeat something when we want to make sure whomever we are communicating with gets the message. So who was this Stephen? He was a disciple chosen by a multitude of people to spread the gospel. He wasn't afraid to be honest, truthful or even frightening. His sole purpose was to reach the lost. He was a normal person like you and me, he just allowed God to use him. *Acts 6:8 "And Stephen, full of faith and power, did great wonders and miracles among the people."*

God can do anything through us if we allow him to. By allowing this we have to believe, and be full of faith and then we can receive the power of God. We can love our enemies with the same love and compassion that God has for us but only through his intervention. We need to begin to pray for God to take over our minds, our hearts and our eyes that we may see others as he sees them. That we may love others as he loves them, and that we may think of others as he thinks of them.

To forgive is a great gift. We need to try to see the soul of a person instead of seeing the shell of the person. When we do this, it won't matter what they have done, the only thing that will matter is who holds their soul in eternity. We can't reach others if we can't love them. We can't love them if we can't forgive them.

Luke 6:32-36 "If you love those who love you, what credit is that to you? Even 'sinners' love those who love them. And if you do good to those who are good to you, what credit is that to you? Even 'sinners' do the same. And if you lend to those from whom you expect repayment, what credit is that to you? Even 'sinners' lend to 'sinners', expecting to be repaid in full. But love your enemies, do good to them, and lend to them without expecting to get anything back. Then your reward will be great, and you will be sons of the Most High, because he is kind to the ungrateful and wicked. Be merciful, just as your Father is merciful."

Forgiving is a learned behavior. It is only given by the one who has perfected it and who is the perfect teacher for those students who are willing to learn. Are you willing to learn how to forgive someone who has had an abortion? Are you willing to learn to love them? Do you want to see them through the eyes of Jesus? If you want to reach the lost you need to be ready for anything, anyone and any circumstance. God is calling all sinners to come home to him no matter what their sin. These women are broken inside and Satan will keep them that way if he can.

It is important to remember that God has a purpose for each of us. He wants the future of every soul, not the past. He can still use each and every one of us and he can utilize whatever baggage we have acquired in this life. Amazing, huh? I find it utterly baffling how awesome he is and how immense his grace is. God wants these women, he wants to fix their brokenness, he wants to raise them up and fill them with joy. He wants to use the talents and gifts that he gave them to reach a part of the world that someone else may never be able to reach.

God planned each one of these women just as he planned you. He works out every detail of our decisions, good and bad, into the purpose of his will. *Ephesians 1:11 "In him we were also chosen, having been predestined according to the plan of him who works out everything in conformity with the purpose of his will."* If you are fighting ill feelings you may have towards these women or anyone, you will never reach them for the Lord. People will only open up with someone they feel they can trust, they have faith in and they believe.

If you can ask God to give you the ability to love someone who has aborted a baby and you actually allow him to work in your life, you can be a tool God uses to reach these women. A simple hug or look of compassion and a kind word may be all that is needed. They will begin to trust you, share their struggles and fears and they will believe what you tell them because you care, because you are safe. If you tell them who your God is and what he can do in their life, you may find a calling you never imagined. Watching a soul being set free from a sinful bondage is by far the greatest experience anyone could ever encounter. You may feel more fulfilled and closer to God than you ever thought you could. This is a mission field! Loving is the key to forgiveness and forgiveness is the key to the heart of God. *Proverbs 10:12 "Hatred stirs up dissension, but love covers all wrongs."*

Chapter 5

Forgiving Myself

Forgiveness— the act of excusing a mistake or an offense; readiness to forgive.

Understanding the realm of God's forgiveness is something we can not comprehend. God has no limitations; it is our sin and lack of conscience or awareness that has created boundaries in our understanding of true forgiveness. Until we are released from the sin, the boundaries cannot be removed. Being released of some sins requires much more than we are ready for. Simply asking God's forgiveness isn't enough if we haven't first prepared ourselves. So how do we do that? What does that even mean? It may sound confusing but in reality it is very simple. In my own personal experience and the experiences others who have freely shared with me, I believe there are three basic reasons we find ourselves in this state.

1. We are unsure that we have been forgiven because when we have asked God to forgive us, we don't feel any different. Or, we feel better initially but later come back to the same guilt and shame as before.
2. We don't recognize our faults or sins therefore we do not feel that we are bad enough to require anymore forgiveness.
3. We don't believe there is enough we can do to have real forgiveness. We feel we have to physically work for it and we find that impossible and exhausting. (We don't believe we should be forgiven.)

As we look at each of these individually, ask God to help you be aware if any apply to you. This is not a time to point out how others you know might need to read this. It is meant for you just as it meant for me. Open your mind up to the possibility of what you may need to hear. I know it isn't easy but the blessing is always magnificent.

We are unsure that we have been forgiven because when we have asked God to forgive us, it just doesn't seem to be happening, we don't feel any different.

Has this ever happened to you? You feel

convicted of something, it eats at you and finally you go to God and ask his forgiveness. Oddly enough, you know you asked forgiveness but the pain or conviction doesn't seem to go away. We then began to ask ourselves if we are really forgiven and if we aren't, why?

Here it is, what I was referring to earlier, the part we may not be prepared for. As I have come to face my own demons, I have learned much about God. One thing I have learned which has been almost solely responsible for the change in my life, is how much God truly loves me. I have broken every commandment, I have disappointed my family, my friends, myself, and most importantly God by choices I have made in my life. I believed for many years that I was unforgiveable. Still to this day, I am truly humbled and honored by how God could still want me. How he could actually want to use me. As I write this I remember asking God to take away the pain of some of my choices. I remember wanting God to help me forget or take me back so I could make the right choices. I asked God over and over again to forgive me but I never really felt it. What I finally figured out was that I couldn't move past it because I had never forgiven myself. You see, God could not forgive me because I could not forgive myself. I had created a boundary which kept God from being able to give me forgiveness and because of this boundary God was not able to use me for his purpose either.

God can only do great things through us if we allow him too. I believed that I was unworthy but as I began to really get into my Bible and set aside space in my schedule for God everyday he began to work in me. Over time my thoughts and actions changed and I realized that I had something to offer. I realized that God created me knowing that I would someday face my choices and knowing the choices I would make. I thought about David and how he was a man after God's own heart. He was a murderer, an adulterer and a liar but God used him in a mighty way. God loved him in a mighty way, even with all his baggage. David too had to forgive himself for what he did and he understood that.

Forgiveness of sin is always a two-way process. You can not have it without God granting it and you cannot receive it without accepting it. I believe that the greatest gift outside of salvation God has ever given us is the gift of sharing. In everything we do with our Father we must do it together. If we draw near to him, he will draw near to us. **James 4:8**. He knocks on our hearts door and waits for us to open it. **Revelation 3:20**. You see, everything is shared with our Savior. He doesn't just want to be Lord; he wants to be our Father, our friend, our protector, our provider, our rescuer and our greatest love.

If you want real forgiveness, prime yourself to receive it. Ask your Father to help you understand what you have done and accept that it can not be undone. Ask him to help you grasp that you are not unforgiveable nor are you forgotten. Be real with God when you are talking with him. He already knows your thoughts, your feelings, all of them, good and bad. He wants to be intimate with you but he can't unless you get real by verbally sharing the pain, the anger, the why's of whatever you are holding on too. Whether it is abortion, a failed marriage, abuse of any kind, rape, financial difficulties, death of a loved one, whatever you are facing, he needs you to be real about it. It is only when you cry out to him in genuine sincerity of your feelings that you really get to know him. It is also in these times that he shapes and molds you into his likeness.

If you are reading this and know this is the step you need to take to find a peace about your past and a hope for your future, stop right here, find a private place where you can scream, or cry or let go in whatever way you need too. Your Father is waiting for you; he is holding out his arms and longing for you to run into them.

We do not recognize our faults or our sin therefore we do not require anymore forgiveness.

This is a very difficult area to discuss. It is difficult because most people do not want to evaluate their own lives in fear of what they might find. We are all the same, we want to be right, we feel we are decent people and therefore we are okay in our spiritual walk. Every one of us at some point has laid some poor individual on the sacrificial table of ridicule and judgment. Yes, all of us!

I recall getting out of the car one day at the local Walgreens store, glancing across the parking lot when I saw this woman. She was a very large woman wearing short shorts and a tank top. It was very difficult not to notice her but when I think about my reaction I am ashamed. I thought…"Oh My Goodness!!! What is she thinking, that is so awful!" Not only did I think it, I brought it to my friend's attention as well. Why? Because somehow I thought I was better than her. I was better because I didn't dress like that. What I should have done was try to look a bit deeper. For some reason she wanted this attention. What was she missing in her life that she would deliberately bring negative attention to herself? Did she even realize that the attention she was getting was negative? All I do know is that she was crying out for someone to see her.

Have we not all had moments like this? Sometimes we actually get into an attitude that we have the right to behave this way. We are saved, we are "CHRISTIANS" and we think that makes this okay. It doesn't. It most certainly doesn't make God proud of us. When I think of how I was in the same place at the same time as that woman in the parking lot, I now wonder if that was a test. You see, there are no accidents. I believe that day God bowed his head in shame of me. I know tears ran down his face as he watched me treat her badly. Whether she knew him or not, I would never have seen it because I was too wrapped up in how she looked to see anything else.

What about you? Stop and think about the last time you spoke of someone else in a negative way. Are you asking yourself what this all has to do with forgiveness? Well...it has everything to do with it. If we feel that as followers of Christ we can behave this way the odds are that we are blind to our spiritual life. If we are blind to our walk with God, we are numb to conviction and we are no longer moving forward. This means that we can not find forgiveness because we do not believe that we need it. The truth lies in one verse that we must always remember. *Romans 3:23 "For all have sinned and fall short of the glory of God."* Salvation doesn't make us worthy, it makes us saved. We should look at our lives every day and ask God to help us oil any area that is getting a bit rusty. We are human which means that we will sin every day. This also means that every day we need to come back to God thanking him for his grace and asking him to help us adjust those areas that we fail in. *Lamentations 3:40 "Let us examine our ways and test them, and let us return to the Lord."*

The first step is to see where we are. Are we treating others badly with our words? Are we gossiping about things that we shouldn't? Are we embracing bitter feelings because of a situation with another person? Don't look at what they have done or haven't done, look at yourself. God can not use you if you refuse to see your own faults. In fact, Satan will use you to destroy what God is trying to build.

What I have learned is that I am not better than any soul on this earth. I am not worthy of the salvation that was offered to me and because of that

I wanted to serve out of thankfulness. I have learned that if I give my life and my time to God, he will allow me to see others the way he does. I have also learned that if at any time I feel that I am doing everything right, I usually am not.

Christianity is not a religion, a habit or a tradition; it is a way of life. The only way to do it is to be moving forward. I love the phrase 'it is not where you stand but in what direction you are moving'. This is the basis of a believer's life. If we are moving backward, we are not only harming ourselves but most likely others as well. If we are standing in the same place we never grow and God can never use us for anything more. But if we are moving forward, God is changing our thoughts, our reactions, and our words and creating within each of us a gentle spirit that welcomes others. Forgiveness breeds these life changing characteristics so never think you do not need forgiveness. Never become complacent, it too will breed as well, but what it breeds is spiritual disaster. Even Paul, one of the greatest teachers and writers of the word told the church of Corinth that he died daily. **I Corinthians 15:31**. If God has convicted you stop right here and talk to him. He convicts you because he loves you. Ask him to show you what areas he wants to shape into his likeness. Ask him to forgive you and help you to move forward. Ask him to help you understand humility, the way Jesus understood it. God is waiting for you.

We do not believe there is enough we can do to have real forgiveness.

Have you ever done something so awful that you do not believe it is forgivable? If so, you and I are very much alike. I worked myself to death in the church trying to feel like I could actually be forgiven depending how much I did for God. When the light bulb came on for me, I finally understood that all that work couldn't do anything for my soul.

I ache for those of you who feel this way. In preparation for this book I met so many that feel they will never nor could ever be given the gift of forgiveness. Let me say to you that if you believe this it is a lie of Satan. He knows the guilt that you carry and he knows that he can use it to hold onto you. He whispers to you that God will never love you, never be able to use you. He tells you the same lie that he told Moses to keep him from saving the Israelites. Remember? Moses killed a man and ran. He was gone from Egypt for many years when God told him to go back and bring his people out of bondage. Satan told Moses he was unworthy, he couldn't do it. Thank goodness Moses didn't listen.

Satan never changes. He uses the same lies over and over again. Paul killed many Christians, yet God used him in a more powerful way than even Peter who walked on water with Jesus. Whatever you have done, if it is brought to the Lord with a genuine desire to be forgiven, it will be forgiven. You can not change yesterday but you can let God change the course of today.

I too thought God could never use me. I argued with him for years over this book. How could I ever speak to anyone about anything after the choices I have made? Why would I ever want anyone to know something so awful about me? And if I did how could God use that? Well, after a long bit of wrestling, God has won and this experience has been amazing. I have been able to reach people I would have never been able to reach if I had kept doing nothing.

There were two important steps I had to take. First, I had to forgive myself. This was the hardest part for me. I will never forget what I have done but I know now that God can use it to help others. Second, I had to really give this to God. This part didn't seem so hard once self-forgiveness had taken place. I can not describe the peace that came over me nor can I explain the change in my behavior. I can only chalk it up to a Father who loves me and kept his promises as always. If God had a plan for someone like me, I know he has a greater plan for someone as special as you.

The day that I finally understood how much God loved me, was the day my life changed. It was the day I found the hope of living for something real. It was the first day of the rest of my life. I want to share with you a letter that aided in the rescue of my spiritual life. To this day, I keep a copy and I read it when I feel unloved or undeserving. It is for me and for anyone who has made the wrong choices in this life a most important letter. It may be hard at first but don't stop reading it. You will not regret it.

Take a moment before you begin and pray. God is with you, he is wrapping his arms around you and kissing your cheek just as a Father does. He loves you so much and he simply wants you to know that. There is nothing that you have done that is unforgiveable, nothing!

My Child,

You may not know me, but I know everything about you...Psalm 139:1. **I know when you sit down and when you rise up**...Psalm 139:2. **I am**

familiar with all your ways...Psalm 139:3. **Even the very hairs on your head are numbered**...Matthew 10:29-31. **For you were made in my image**...Genesis 1:27. **In me you live and move and have your being**...Acts 17:28. **For you are my offspring**...Acts 17:28. **I knew you even before you were conceived**...Jeremiah 1:4-5. **I chose you when I planned creation**...Ephesians 1:11-12. **You were not a mistake**...Psalm 139:15-16. **I determined the exact time of your birth and where you would live**...Acts 17:26. **You are fearfully and wonderfully made**...Psalm 130:14. **I knit you together in your mother's womb**...Psalm 139:13. **And brought you forth on the day you were born**...Psalm 71:6. **I have been misinterpreted by those who do not know me**...John 8:41-44. **I am not distant and angry, but am the complete expression of love**...I John 4:16. **It is my desire to lavish my love on you**...I John 3:1. **Simply because you are my child and I am your Father**...I John 3:1. **I offer you more than your earthly father ever could**...Matthew 7:11. **For I am the perfect Father**...Mathew 5:48. **Every good gift that you receive comes from my hand**...James 1:17. **For I am your provider and I meet all your needs**...Matthew 6:31-33. **My plan** for your future has always been filled with hope...Jeremiah 29:11. **Because I love you with an everlasting love**...Jeremiah 31:3. **My thoughts toward you are as countless as the sands on the seashore**...Psalm 139:17-18. **And I rejoice over you with singing**...Zephaniah 3:17. **I will never stop doing good to you**...Jeremiah 32:40. **For you are my treasured possession**...Exodus 19:5. **I desire to establish you with all my heart and with all my soul**...Jeremiah 32:41. **And I want to show you great and marvelous things**...Jeremiah 33:3. **If you seek me with all your heart you will find me**...Deuteronomy 4:29. **Delight in me and I will give you the desires of your heart**...Psalm 37:4. **For it is I who gave you those desires**...Philippians 2:13. **I am able to do more for you than you could possibly imagine**...Ephesians 3:20. **For I am your greatest encourager**...II Thessalonians 2:16-17. **I am also the Father who comforts you in all your troubles**...II Corinthians 1:3-4. **When you are broken-hearted, I am close to you**...Psalm 34:18. **As a shepherd carries a lamb, I have carried you close to my heart**...Isaiah 40:11. **One day I will wipe away every tear from your eyes**...Revelation 21:3-4. **And I will take away all the pain you have**

suffered on this earth...Revelation 21:4. **I am your Father and I love you even as I love my son Jesus**...John 17:23. **For in Jesus my love for you is revealed**...John 17:26. **He is the exact representation of my being**...Hebrews 1:3. **And he came to demonstrate that I am for you, not against you**...Romans 8:31. **And to tell you that I am not counting your sins**...II Corinthians 5:18-19. **Jesus died so that you and I could be reconciled**...II Corinthians 5:18-19. **His death was the ultimate expression of my love for you**...I John 4:10. **I gave up everything I love that I might gain your love**...Romans 8:32. **If you receive the gift of my son Jesus, you receive me**...I John 2:23. **And nothing will ever separate you from my love again**...Romans 8:38-39. **Come home and I will throw the biggest party Heaven has ever seen**...Luke 15:7. **I have always been your Father and will always be your Father**...Ephesians 3:14-15. **My question is...Will you be my child?**...John 1:12-13. **I am waiting for you**...Luke 15:11-32.

Love,
Your Dad,
Almighty God

Chapter Six

Abortion Prevention Step 1:

Know Who Satan Is

Sometimes in this life, we forget that God is not the only powerful being that is unseen or invisible to us. I sometimes think we don't want to believe that Satan is real or what we are told he is capable of is not an actuality in this life; but it is. As parents we believe that God will protect our children but what we think he should protect them from may be pointless if we can't comprehend the truth of what is around us.

We ask God to keep our children safe from harm, to keep them away from being led down the wrong path or for God to heal their ailments. These are all wonderful things to pray for, I pray for them too but can we go deeper? To God are these prayers enough or is he saying to us, it's so much bigger than that? We need to understand that Satan is there, lurking, waiting and timing his attacks on our children at just the precise moment. He is powerful in his own right and he knows things about our children that we don't even know. He uses that knowledge to feed them, to feed their mind with false garbage from violent music to sexually explicit movies. To feed their bodies with 'feel good' moments that consists of drugs, sex, and alcohol. He feeds their need for motivation and acceptance with people that we probably wouldn't approve of.

God tells us everything we need to know about Satan through the scriptures. He warns us of who he is and what he can do. We as believers must have an unobstructed view of this truth. As I began to look at this from a new perspective, it became profoundly clear to me that I truly had no idea of the fight that was taking place all around my children between good and evil. It encompasses us; it's all around us all the time. In what we watch, where we go, what we see and who we befriend. It can impact us to such an extent that it takes over our thought process which is the starting point for temptation. Think about it, when you see the cover of a DVD box at the movie store that is graphically sexual, does it not stir something in your mind?

Satan's influence is everywhere, just waiting to conquer our children and take their souls. If we don't really believe this, we are living in Satan's matrix. Have you seen the movie, The Matrix? I did many years ago and it stuck with me in the sense that this world is governed by the same rules. Agent Smith and all his friends hunted those whose minds were freed from their prison. Those who were still stuck in the matrix were of no concern to the agents, they weren't a threat. They were only concerned with those who knew and understood what was real. Remind you of anyone, maybe...Satan? Mr. Smith knew that Morpheus and his team would continue to free the minds and souls of others. They became Agent Smith's sole purpose; to steal, kill and destroy them. This brings to mind *John 10:10a "The thief comes only to steal, kill and destroy;"*

Remember when Neo was set free? Before he could re-enter the matrix he had to train, learn what was real and what was not, and refocus his entire being on bringing freedom to all he could. Just like Neo and his friends there are only few believers who truly understand and grasp this reality. I realize that the movie may not have intended any spiritual or godly implications but for me, I found the similarities fantastical.

There is only one place we should want to be and just like Morpheus, Trinity and Neo; it is Zion. Coincidence? Who knows, but it is most definitely ironic. Zion is the chosen place of God. It is where he resides and where we should desire to be. *Psalm 9:11 "Sing praises to the Lord, enthroned in Zion: proclaim among the nations what he has done."*

How do I know all of this? What makes me an expert? I am not an expert, I am not Dr. Phil's protégé and I am not a psychologist. I have no degree in counseling or sociology, I didn't even graduate from college. I am a woman who believes in the Word of God and has been forgiven much. I am woman who can never repay my debt nor deserves the unfailing love of a mighty God. I am a woman who believes that all of the answers to this life are in the Holy Bible. That doesn't make me an expert, it makes God the expert.

There are three scriptures we should look at very closely.

1. II Corinthians 12:7 Satan is the tormentor!

"To keep me from becoming conceited because of these surpassingly great revelations, there was given me a thorn in my flesh, a messenger of Satan, to torment me."

This was Paul talking to the Corinthians of how he could become conceited because of all that had happened during his ministry. God allowed Satan to torment him and to make him weak. If Paul was weak he would have to cry out to God for strength. God knows if everything were wonderful in our lives than we wouldn't need him or we wouldn't think we needed him. This is why he has given Satan permission to torment us.

Do you need to reread that last line? **God has given Satan permission to torment us**.

This doesn't mean God doesn't love us. He allows it to bring us freedom in our choices and to keep us close to him because he loves us. So what is my point? Our children have a permanent thorn in their side. It isn't you as their parents, it isn't their little brother or sister; it is Satan himself! He is utilizing this permission and pushing it to the max every time. We must also remember that God will not allow Satan to tempt us beyond that which we can handle and he always gives us a way out.

I Corinthians 10:13 "No temptation has seized you except what is common to man. And God is faithful; he will not let you be tempted beyond what you can bear. But when you are tempted, he will also provide a way out so that you can stand up under it."

Temptation is part of the torment. It is the starting point and none of us are safe from it. We can bear it through God's strength but only when we are prepared. Are your children prepared to fight?

Are you starting to see how this works? If you knew that there was some stranger watching your child, lurking behind bushes and vacant buildings, just waiting for a chance to hurt them, what would you do? You would do everything humanly possible to protect them. Well, it is happening and we need to do everything **spiritually** possible to protect them.

2. Revelation 12:9 Satan leads the world astray!

"The great dragon was hurled down that ancient serpent called the devil, or Satan, who leads the whole world astray"

I believe this scripture is significant because it is very matter of fact. Here he is, Satan, he leads the whole world astray. There is no beating around the bush. This is God's warning to us. It doesn't say he only leads half astray, it says he leads the whole world astray. Whole is complete, meaning all. In this scripture he is telling us that Satan's sole purpose and passion is to lead us away from our Heavenly Father, and ensure our place in the depths of hell with him. He doesn't care if it is the President of the United States or Joe's daughter at the diner down the road. Neither God nor the devil see the prestige of persons in this life. They see only our souls. Satan is definitely going to hell and he knows it, and he is taking with him all that he can and our children are his prey.

Satan knows who we are, who our children are if we serve the Lord. There is a scripture that brought this home to me as I was reading in Acts. It tells the story of men who were proclaiming to cast out demons in the name of Christ when Paul was passing through Ephesus. *Acts 19:13-16 "Some Jews who went around driving out evil spirits tried to invoke the name of the Lord Jesus over those who were demon-possessed. They would say, "In the name of Jesus, whom Paul preaches, I command you to come out." Seven sons of Sceva, a Jewish chief priest, were doing this. One day, the evil spirit answered them, "Jesus I know and I know about Paul, but who are you? Then the man who had the evil spirit jumped on them and overpowered them all. He gave them such a beating that they ran out of the house naked and bleeding."*

Whoa, did that not give you goose pimples? Did you really think about what you just read? First of all, a demon who possessed a man spoke to these men who were not believers. I would think that alone would cause serious brain signals to channel the freak out and run for your life mode. I can't honestly say my first reaction wouldn't be a bit on the "AHHHHHHHHHH!!!!!!!!!!!!!!!! Side. How bout you? But the scariest part is what the demon said to them. The demon knew Jesus and Paul because of their faith but he didn't know these men because they weren't believers. Do you get it? If Satan has you, he doesn't even care to know you; he only wants your soul. Sound a bit like Agent Smith? If you are not a threat you are not causing any glitches to the devils plan. If however, you have been freed from his prison of sin, he makes certain that he not only knows you by name but everything about you. He is determined to get you and he won't stop!

3. Luke 4:5-13—Satan knows the Word of God is powerful!

""The devil led him up to a high place and showed him in an instant all the kingdoms of the world. And he said to him, "I will give you all their authority and splendor, for it has been given to me, and I can give it to anyone I want to. So if you worship me, it will all be yours." Jesus answered "It is written: Worship the

73

Lord your God and serve him only." The devil led him to Jerusalem and had him stand on the highest point of the temple. "If you are the Son of God," he said, "Throw yourself down from here. For it is written: He will command his angels concerning you to guard you carefully; they will lift you up in their hands, so that you will not strike your foot against a stone." Jesus answered, "It says: Do not put the Lord your God to the test. When the devil had finished all this tempting, he left him until an opportune time."

Okay, this tells us everything about the devil. First of all, he is tempting the Son of God!—HELLO!!!—What was he thinking? He was offering Jesus worldly power. Did you see where the devil stated that all that power had been given to him and he could give it to whomever he wanted? Do we still have any questions about what Satan can or can't do? He can give us illnesses, take our children's innocence, put us into famine, destroy our marriages and so much more. On the same hand, he can offer money, success, romance, beauty, and material items beyond our belief. He has that kind of dominion over this world.

So was the devil thinking that if he was bold enough to tempt the Son of God, Jesus just might crack? NOT! If he thought he could sway the Son of

God, there is no way he will hold back on our families, our marriages or our children. Thank goodness Jesus was the perfect man, the man without sin, the perfect and holy sacrifice. Thank goodness that he knew his purpose and was not swayed by the tormentor. What Jesus was, was prepared. He knew Satan would try and he knew that Satan would keep trying. He also knew that Satan could quote scripture word for word. So how do we fight the likes of Satan and his posse? We get in the Word and we know the Word. We fight it just as Jesus did. We must read and study and ask God to guide and direct us in not only comprehending the scripture the way God intended, but to hide it in our heart so that we are always prepared to battle the devil.

We all know how hard it is to swim against a current. It is hard for us to stay on the straight and narrow pathway in our own personal relationship with God. If we have trouble as adults, how much harder is it for our kids? Most of us as parents, did not face the level of temptation and perversions that our children are faced with today. Some of these kids are walking through metal detectors, hoping that some crazed student isn't going to open fire before they graduate. That is a whole new level of worries, something that may be very hard to for us to conceive. We may have walked five miles to school but we weren't afraid we wouldn't come home.

You see, the world is this huge current of mile high tides that come in and drown our kids. They barely have time to catch their breath before the next tide rolls in. They are beat up day after day by the ugliness of the world. They want to be accepted and popular, they need to feel important. There is only so much beating they can take before they give in and Satan is counting on it.

If we can grasp who Satan is and what he is capable of, we may have a chance to help our children. If we chose to live in Satan's matrix we will never be able to offer them any protection. In fact, we may, without realizing it, assist the devil in his quest. You don't have to believe me, I don't want you to take my word for it, take God's Word for it!

Chapter Seven

Prevention Step 2: Know Who Your Children Are

They are Sinners!

Romans 3:23 "For all have sinned and fall short of the glory of God."

When we look at our children we see them in a different respect than the children of others. Of course we do, they are **our** children. They are part of us, part of our DNA, we have raised them, loved them and cared for them. So the bottom line is that we are biased. I have to admit that I am. I think my children are the cutest, funniest, most amazing children ever! Don't we all? We have to be very careful though because this can cause us to become blinded to who they truly are and what can happen to them in this place called our world.

Who they truly are:

They are sinners just like you!!! They were born into sin like everyone else and they are vulnerable to attack just as you and I are. They are not protected from that even though we want to believe that they are. Think back to times in your life when you did something that you either said you would never do, thought you would never do or promised you would never do. Something that you feel ashamed for now but at the time it didn't seem so terrible. We have all been there. Some are worse than others on our scale but the point here is that if we did it, what in the world makes us think that our kids won't? If we were tempted and tormented by Satan what makes us think that our kids won't be?

For **ALL** have sinned! **ALL** fall short of God's glory! We have to come to the understanding that we alone cannot protect our children every moment of every day. We have to accept that Satan is waiting for the very instant we are not there. We have to understand that the things they don't talk to us about, Satan knows about it and he will use it to temp and torment them. He will tell them lies, he will whisper sweet nothings to them with promises of giving them everything they want. He will use whatever means necessary to get the job done, including parents.

There is one thing I have come to accept and that is that both our creator and the devil use other people to accomplish their goals. If you have a teenager or a child that has been through the teenage phase, do you ever recall a time in which they became friends with someone you didn't approve or were uncomfortable with? Did your teen seem to begin behaving differently? Well, this is what I am talking about. Satan was using that friend to influence your child. So how then could he use us as parents? If we saw these things and did nothing than we also were aiding in his ultimate goal. God uses us as well. He expects us to be aware of what is going on with our children and create a roadblock if they are veering toward the wrong path. The bottom line? We as parents are helping one or the other.

Have you ever encountered someone that said their child would never have sex before marriage? Oopps...it often seems that it is their children who do. I have more than once, experienced very proud 'Christians', those who tend to judge the harshest and what I have found is their children always seem to find a way to humble them. The point? Don't let Satan tempt you to believe that your child is somehow excluded from evil. They are not! It may be hard to believe, but when you accept this you will be able to help your child become a well rounded and moral human being. The key is to know who the tormentor is and how powerful he can be when he chooses too.

They are tempted and hunted!
Hebrews 4:15 *"For we do not have a high priest who is unable to sympathize with our weaknesses, but we have one who has been tempted in every way, just as we are—yet was without sin."*

Can you imagine never sinning? To think that out of every human being ever born into this world, only one was without sin. He wasn't sinless because he wasn't tempted, he was sinless because he was the only soul capable of not falling into temptation. That didn't stop the devil though, he still tried, even on the Son of God. No one is safe from Satan!

We come back to this reality that our children are prey. It is hard to think this way, at least for me. As I try to wrap my mind around this it makes me think of a most beautiful animal, the deer. A doe tries to protect her fawn because she knows that it is vulnerable. She tries to avoid open fields if at all possible merely because she grasps that her fawn is exposed and defenseless and knows that the fawn doesn't understand that about itself. Amazing isn't it? We must have the insight to realize our children are like the does fawn, exposed and defenseless and most importantly understand that they don't know it. We must have the wisdom, patience and strength to help them. How do we do this? We start by accepting that our children will fail because they will sin. They will sin because they are not perfect and they are not perfect because they are our children. Are you perfect? Have you never sinned? Think of the worst thing in your life you have ever done and imagine that your son or daughter will do the same, maybe worse. I bet that changes things a bit. It most certainly did for me.

Jesus Christ was the most humble and caring man that ever walked this earth. He was the full expression of God the Father and the ultimate sacrifice. On the day of his physical death, God had to look away because he could not bear to see the sin. It is this very incident between Jesus and the Father that makes me know my children are in danger. What I mean is that if God allowed Satan to tempt his only son in every way so that he could bear the sin of the world, why...why...why...would we ever even consider the notion that our children are safe? Only the Bible tells us the truth. *I Peter 5:8*

"Be self controlled and alert. Your enemy the devil prowls around like a roaring lion looking for someone to devour."

If we are wise parents, we must try to see that our children are Satan's prey. Everyday they are tempted to misbehave, to lie, to steal, cheat or harm themselves or someone else; whether physically, emotionally or mentally. Being aware of this will make us better parents. We are not their friend, we are their guide.

They are weak!

Hebrews 5:2 "He is able to deal gently with those who are ignorant and are going astray, since he himself is subject to weakness."

Jesus weak? Was that possible? Of course it was because he was human. He could not have been the perfect sacrifice had he not been weak and tempted. On the flip side of this, if he was weak and never sinned, how weak does that make us?

If thinking of your children or loved one as weak is hard than think of them as fragile. Life is funny when you think of the irony of how it works. A young person doesn't seem weak, they seem fit, strong and motivated, yet they are fragile. An elderly person seems fragile, breakable, unhealthy and tired, yet they are wise. So how does that work? It isn't physical it is mental.

Everything in this life we think, feel, and do is all a reaction to our mental state. How many times have we become angry and said or done something in that moment of anger that we regret? Something that we may never have thought we would have done? Our mind is our greatest and most dangerous asset. It takes years to train it, mold it and teach it what it knows. This explains the older and wiser, younger fragile theory. Here's an example that I found rather amusing. My best friend was visiting for the weekend with her two girls and we were preparing to fix dinner. When I suggested seafood she curled her nose up and said, me and my kids won't eat that. My response was that my children and I loved it. The point is that she did not like it and her children had grown not to like it because their entire life they heard her say it wasn't good. Even if they tried it they had already decided in their mind it tasted bad. On the other hand, I loved it and my children had heard it was good their entire life, therefore, they liked it too.

Our children or nieces, nephews, grandchildren are mentally growing and this is where they are vulnerable and exposed. Of course the physical side is a factor but we already know what will happen there. They will grow to be an adult size in the physical sense. It is the mind that we don't know about. As they grow, we don't know what they are thinking about, what they are dreaming about or what they are longing for. We can not measure the maturity of their mind like we can the maturity of their physical size. I have met ten year olds that can blow me away in math. They are more mature than I am when it comes to understanding numbers. However, when it comes to paying bills they don't have a clue. I don't have to know algebra to pay my bills. I have to know how to manage my life to pay my bills and be able to survive until payday comes back around. They don't understand that because they haven't been taught yet. Based on how they see their parents do this will most likely impact how they do it. It is all about the mind!

This brings us back to the fact that we are all weak, especially our children. We must build the strength of their mind and what we teach them through how we live. We must protect what they see, what they read and what they watch. Jesus was vulnerable to weakness because he had a human mind. This is where all temptation begins and is born.

We must embrace the absolute fact that our sons and daughters are mentally exposed and vulnerable to the attacks of Satan every moment of every day. This is where they are the weakest and if we are not providing them with the right mental diet so to speak, they will have a very difficult time fighting an unhealthy thought process. The truth is that we can not help them or teach them if we can not see that there is an issue. Have I forgotten about abortion? No, but how will you ever protect your child from having pre-marital sex or having an abortion if you don't believe they could do it?

We must open our minds to the reality that the only way we can truly protect our younger generation is through the Creator. Through prayer and most importantly through actually living what we teach them. Can we protect them from having premarital sex? Yes, I believe we can but only if we are honest with ourselves and with the fact that they will be tempted and can fall into sexual immorality. If they fail there, can we stop them from making a life changing and devastating decision to abort? I believe that we can. We must be open and honest with our children, talk to them, don't be afraid. We must let them know that we will love them. We must embrace discipline as a parent in our actions with our children just as our Father shows to us. *Proverbs 29:17 "Discipline your son, and he will give you peace; he will bring delight to your soul."*

Chapter Eight

Prevention Step 3:

Doing Life with God

We say we are believers but do we really live that lifestyle? I used to think that I did until I really got into the Word of God and realized that I was far from it. Doing life with God is by far one of the greatest and most rewarding lifestyles anyone could ever encounter. Life is a chain of events. Some are good, some are bad and some are just ugly but no matter what the situation, if you're sharing it with God, you have found freedom.

At the church my family attended for several years until our recent move our pastor preached a message that has been with me everyday since. It was about God being first in everything in our lives. The way Pastor John laid it out literally changed my life. For the first time I actually understood what I *wasn't* doing right. Through scripture he showed me how God should be my first thought in the morning. God should receive the first portion of my time everyday. He should get the first of the income my family is provided. God should be the first person I talk to about a decision or situation. All of these things should happen before anything or anyone else. I decided that day that I was going to make him my first and that was the day I started doing life with God. God began to bless me in ways that I didn't even understand. My family started talking about the change in my attitude and behavior. I didn't worry about things anymore; I had a peace that was not about one thing in particular it was a peace about everything.

The most important part of that process of God taking over my mind and my life was the testimony that was created for my husband and children. I remember the day my husband came into the kitchen as I was making breakfast. He leaned over, kissed me and then he just smiled and starred at me. I asked him why he was looking at me like that and he said the most wonderful thing. "You really are different, aren't you?" I knew exactly what he meant and it was the most amazing compliment anyone could have ever given me. I was so surprised because up to that point I hadn't noticed anything drastically different about myself. I just knew I was happy. After that event I realized how God was using my life as an encouragement in theirs.

I use that story because it is our lifestyle that either encourages or discourages a relationship with God to those around us. The fact is there is no in between in that. I used to just preach about how we should live our lives and my family's response was to ignore me. Why? Because I didn't practice what I preached. Even now, there are days that I miss the boat and when I miss spending time with God I am not as patient or loving in my reactions to those around me. The funny thing is that my family is so much more accepting of those days because they know that I am trying, I am really trying.

On the days that I don't do life with God, I don't get all the help I need to be that person that I can only be with God. You see, doing life with God is so much more than talking about it or never missing a church service. It is real, everyday encounters with our creator. We can never reach people through our words, in most cases we do more damage than good when we speak about our beliefs. However, we can begin to reach people and encourage them to seek

God by making a choice to share our lives with God.
As we go through this chapter we also have to remember that we are still human and being human means we are not perfect. We will still make mistakes and we will still sin everyday. That is just how it is. I do ignorant human things just like everyone else. Unfortunately, sometimes even in my effort to do good or avoid a situation I make things worse. This always happens when I don't pray about something first. Always pray first!!!!

Why do I share these stories of my failures as a believer? I share them because each one is a learning tool for me and I hope that each reader can learn from them as well. I also want to be sure that it is understood that I struggle through this life just like everyone else. Writing a book doesn't make you an expert and it sure doesn't make you perfect. Use my mistakes so you can avoid these situations in your own life. As I am coming to the close of this book project I dare say that I will make more senseless decisions that I may regret, because I am human. Remember, being saved doesn't make us worthy or perfect, it just makes us saved.

There are three steps we can take that I believe could be a great benefit to how teenagers or young adults will respond when it comes to a sensitive issue. This could include sex, abortion, alcohol, drugs, eating disorders, self-cutting or any other situation a young person may be facing today. Please remember that this is not judgment or condemnation for anything anyone is currently doing it is just suggestions. After working closely with teenagers, listening to their problems and feelings and working with women, most of whom had abortions in their teen or young adult years, these steps could be crucial. Doing life with God is most important in utilizing these steps correctly. The bond between these steps and living a godly life is not only necessary, it is imperative.

Step 1: Accept your own failures and *do not* push them off your children.

Have you ever been there? You did something that you regret and you fear that your child will do the same? Maybe you don't fear it you know they will do it. You smoked, you think they will. You drank, you think they will. You had sex before you were married, you think they will. I could go on and on with examples but I won't. I think we all understand the meaning. I can not begin to describe to you how many times I have heard a teenager share with me the burden of this very problem. However, there are two sides to this issue and we will look at both as we go through this chapter.

There are many different ways that we as parents push our failures off on our children. I listed some above but what about in other areas of our lives? I know of young people who feel burdened because they have to be the best soccer player, quarterback, artist, singer, or parent because it is expected of them. Then you hear them say they don't understand because their parent wasn't the best so why do they have to be. In most cases, the parent pushed their child to succeed in an area where they failed because it gives the parent some feeling of accomplishment. The problem is that this causes numerous reactions of rebellion, bitterness and hurt within the child. When this happens there can be horrific consequences for both parties.

Let me get right down to it and bring all of that jibber-jabber down to earth. Just because you did something doesn't mean that your children will do the same. If you constantly make them feel that way they will most likely fulfill your fears out of desperation only because they know you expect nothing else. They will feel that no matter what they do it will never be enough to please you and will eventually give up the fight.

This is a place you don't want to be when it comes to your children. When this happens it creates a barrier that in some cases will never go away. Even into the adult years your child may forever hold a grudge against you that will keep them from forming a real relationship with you in later years. If you pressure them to be the best at a sport or instrument for example, it may create a fear of failure so that when failure comes, and it will, they can not handle the situation rationally. They will blame others for their bad choices or short comings and you for everything else. I am not saying that you shouldn't encourage them or even push a little. The key is that you are encouraging even when they do not perform at the level you expect.

I recall going to Steak and Shake one afternoon. A man and his son came in and sat in the booth in front of me. It was obvious that they had just come from a soccer game as this little boy wore his uniform covered in mud. I would have guessed the boy to be around 9 years old. As I sat there trying to enjoy my lunch, all I wanted to do was go over and smack the tar out of this man as he was nearly screaming at this young boy. The boy had not met his dad's expectations during the soccer game he had just played so I guess dad felt he needed to push him a little. I remember looking at the face on that youngster and my heart broke. I could see it, he would never be good enough, that is what he was thinking and he was only a child. I bet he would have given anything that day to have his dad tell him it was okay, that we all make mistakes and that there is always another game. Have you ever experienced anything like this? Does it remind you of your mother or father? We tend many times to do what we learned to do by the way our parents raised us. Think long and hard about what you didn't like when you were a kid and do a self check to see where you are with your parenting. We only get one chance as a parent and our children will only get the same one chance with their children. What we do can become a cycle of good or vicious cycle of bad so chose wisely how you react to each situation.

So when do we push? Well, as I said before I am not an expert but it may not be pushing that we need to do. Setting boundaries and standing firm on those boundaries may be the answer. If they have homework, they don't do anything until it is done and you have checked. If they have chores, they do nothing until those chores are completed and you have checked. The key here is to set the boundary and follow through so they know they have to accomplish those tasks.

As parents we do need to push our children to be all that they can be but they are so vulnerable so we have to be careful in how we do this. If we chose to use negativity to pursue the success of our children we will ultimately cause them to fail. Do you use the 'I won't tell them about all the bad things I did' method? This may be even worse than what we just discussed. When kids think their parents were perfect, they will immediately give up trying to please you. Why? Because they can't be perfect. They need to know that you made mistakes just like everyone else. Letting them see that vulnerable side of you as a parent isn't a bad thing, it simply means they know you are human. This whole being a parent thing is a lot more difficult than we ever imagined, isn't it?

So how does this have anything to do with abortion? I am so glad you are wondering because one of the answers given as a reason for abortion is this very thing. Many young women and men feel that their parents are expecting them to fail so they panic, afraid of the "I KNEW YOU WOULD DO THIS!" or "YA KNOW, I'M JUST NOT SURPRISED!" responses given by parents as if they were just sitting around waiting for it to happen. Your kids don't want to give you that satisfaction so the panic mode takes them right to the doors of the abortion clinics simply to dodge the expected disappointment they knew you would have for them. Maybe this happened to you, so what you are going to do to help your child make better choices? If the above is your strategy you might want to rethink it. I have had to rethink my entire parenting process and I am still working on making myself better so I can be a better parent for my children.

Step 2: Be ready to use your mistakes and failures when you must!

This is a sensitive area for many parents or guardians. Why? Because we don't want to share our disasters with anyone let alone our children, right? I completely understand and have many times fought this battle within myself. So why do we have to go down this road sometimes? Just as I stated above, because it may be necessary. It is necessary in order for our children to succeed. As our children begin to come into their own, so to speak, they will make mistakes and bad choices at some point and if they believe that you never made mistakes this will only complicate their choices.

Why? Because they can again, never measure up.

I recall just recently talking with my teenage son. We were talking about a young lady that he was interested in. I asked him if she was kind to others, if she was a good influence and if so, how did he know this. His initial response was that she was very pretty. My response followed with asking if she was just as pretty on the inside as the outside. I began to explain the importance of dating and how dating is only a preliminary step to marriage. Because of this it is so very important to make sure whomever our children chose to date, they chose wisely. To help him understand I shared with him some of the young men that I had dated, the good and bad situations. I shared my choices and mistakes in those situations and the consequences that I had to face in the aftermath of each one. Of course, things such as premarital sex, alcohol, drugs, our behavior and attitude toward others all came into play in this conversation. It was not easy for me to share with him that part of my life and I was careful in how much I shared but I felt it was necessary.

I have learned to swallow my pride when it comes to my children and have many times apologized for my behavior in handling a situation. It is humbling but it has in fact, created a stronger bond with them. They know that I am not afraid to admit when I am wrong. They know I am not afraid to apologize and they know that I am not afraid to be honest, even when they can visibly see that it is hard for me. I do not want my children to know that their mother was a failure in life at times. I want them to know that I have overcome those failures and they cannot know this unless I share with them the truth of who I was and who I am today.

Please do not misunderstand, I am not suggesting that you sit them down and tell them every wrong decision you made along the way or every horrible consequence you encountered. I am simply suggesting that when it applies to the situation your children may be facing you are not afraid to let them know that you have been there and have faced the very same temptations.

Step 3: Let them know you love them even when they fail.

This is one of the most vital steps we must take whether we are a parent, grandparent, pastor or of any influence in the life of a young person. In my experience with all ages I have learned that one of the greatest fears individuals face is the fear of losing the love of those they hold dear. It brings us back to the choice of abortion or any other choice that can bring such great division in human relationships.

Christ is our lifeline to how we are to behave in these very situations. Just as I used the scripture of the woman that had committed adultery and was brought to Jesus, the example he gives us is the answer. He loved her and she was amazed by it. There are countless examples in the New Testament of Jesus loving those who had failed or faltered. It was this love and compassion of Christ that made such an impact in his ministry because he understood what these individuals needed.

I will try to give you an example. A couple of years ago my step daughter came to live with us. She had always been a most important part of our lives although we did not get to spend much time with her as we live nearly 1000 miles apart. We had been given the privilege to have her with us for an entire year and we were very excited about it. Our lifestyle was very different than what she was used too and it was difficult for her to adjust. As I spoke to one of our pastor's about the situation he made a suggestion that completely changed the direction we were heading. He told me that when things took a turn for the worst, in the midst of a disagreement with her, to walk up, whisper in her ear that I love her and walk away. At first, I thought, I don't know about this but I am willing to give it a whirl, and I did. She was speechless. She even followed me asking me why I did that. I just kept on walking. We still had our issues and of course, her being a teenager, that's just part of it, but that day made a great impact. Why? Because she could not understand when she had misbehaved why I would show her love. Of course she didn't, I had never done that before but I was amazed at the effect it had and it began a whole new spin on how I perceived myself as a parent.

Please understand that I am a believer in discipline. If all we do as parents is show love in a loving format we could potentially harm our children so we have to show them love through discipline as well. In fact, we have to find a way to balance them both. However, what we must stay clear of is discipline without love. When our children make a mistake, big or small, we must be prepared to be honest with them about our feelings and our disappointments. We take action by whatever method is suitable, whether it is grounding them from an outing or phone or, depending on the situation something more severe. Then what? Then we hug them, then we encourage them, then we tell them that we love them. Will they be angry with us? There is not a doubt in my mind that mine would but I cannot let that persuade me in doing the job that God has given me to lead my children in the right direction.

This is how God has been in my own life. He has watched me make various mistakes and he has been hurt by many things that I have done. He has disciplined me through consequence and in other ways and if it were not for that discipline I would not be where I am nor would I have a full understanding of God's love for me.

Believe it or not used to be the slogan for Ripley's and I think it still is. We could also use this slogan for discipline. What do I mean? Believe it or not, our kids want discipline! It is how they know we love them. When I was in high school there was a young lady who came to live with us for a while. She was only thirteen at the time yet she had the freedom to live her own life. Her mother never knew where she was or when she would be home and concern didn't seem to be on her priority list either. I once asked her why she would want to live with us when my parents seemed so controlling; her response? That means they care. She only stayed for a time but I dare say she will always remember the time she had with us. The point? We must find a balance between love and discipline. We must be able to not only find that balance but to implement that into our lives with those we influence. If we can do this, and we can through Christ, we will be able to protect our children from many things including pre-marital sex and abortion. As we look further into the steps we can take to be better parents and influences on the lives of others remember that in all we do prayer must play the largest role.

Chapter Nine

Prevention Step 4:

Protection Through Prayer

James 5:13 *"Is any one if you in trouble? He should pray. Is anyone happy? Let him sing songs of praise. Is any one of you sick? He should call the elders of the church to pray over him and anoint him with oil in the name of the Lord. And the prayer offered in faith will make the sick person well; the Lord will raise him up. If he has sinned, he will be forgiven. Therefore confess your sins to each other and pray for each other so that you may be healed. The prayer of a righteous man is powerful and effective."*

Prayer is the most powerful, beautiful, effective, unifying and emotional forms of all communication. We see this in many of the scriptures from Genesis through Revelation. Some of the greatest and most moving of all prayers are in the book of Psalms. When we look at these prayers what do we see? What is that moves us and why? As we take a closer look at this phenomenon we may be amazed at how it can transform our lives and the lives of those around us.

1. What is prayer?

Many of us think or have thought that prayer is something we do when we eat, before we go to bed or when we are in trouble. We often times hear of others that we never thought prayed do that very thing in times of trial. When all hope seems lost prayer seems to be the answer. When we cannot pay our bills we pray for Gods financial blessing. When our marriage is falling apart we pray for God's intervention. When our children or a loved one is ill or facing certain death we pray for God's healing. All of these prayers are petitions to our Heavenly Father and all of us have prayed them at some point or another. If you read the above scripture in it's entirety you will find that we are supposed to do this so don't stop, but is there more to prayer?

I have heard others speak of a prayer life or a prayer warrior but never really understood the

meaning of either. I have heard the scriptures that speak of Jesus and others praying without ceasing and never really understood its reality. I began to do what you might call research on prayer. I wanted to know the answer to what prayer really is.

Where did this research lead me? What was my conclusion? I found out that prayer is not only a request or a petition but its greater purpose is renewing of the mind, the body and the soul. Prayer is our thoughts, our desires, our reactions, our needs, our joys and sorrows all wrapped in God' hands. It is what we watch, what we hear and what we do. It is the beginning and the end of who we are. That is the definition of my research, so now let me share with you what I mean.

Prayer is our only communication with God. It the very breath of our faith and our eternal outcome. You see when we are in constant communication with God our thoughts are on God. Our actions and reactions are directed by God and our desires are God's desires for us.

Constant communication or prayer seemed to be impossible when I thought about it in earlier years. How can I pray constantly when I have to work or be a mother? I can't be on my knees all the time what can I do? What I learned is that I can be

constant communication with God as I listen to encouraging music and I am actually praying to him through song. I can talk to God as I drive to work, I can even pray about my bad hair days. I can stop in a situation and in my mind ask God to give me the words to say or help me to do the right thing at the right time. No one else may know what I am doing but God knows and he hears me. Not only does he hear me but he is filled with joy because that is the kind of relationship he wants with me. Without prayer our spiritual life cannot survive.

Have you ever wondered what believer's did before the Bible? How did they know what God wanted or where did they get their guidance? There was only one way to find their answers...prayer! So what is prayer? It is the very nature of God. It is what will transform an individual from a sinner to salvation. The scripture tells us that you must confess your sins (Romans 10:9)...prayer. The scripture tells that we must bring our requests to God (Philippians 4:6)...prayer. The scripture tell us that we must pray without ceasing. *I Thessalonians 5:16-18 "Be joyful always; pray continually; give thanks in all circumstances, for this is God's will for you in Christ Jesus."*

Prayer is always thinking on godly things, always striving to say and do what would make God proud, always asking for guidance in everything, and I mean everything. When you go to the store and purchase groceries, ask God to help you only get those things you need. Talk to him in your mind as you shop, you will be amazed at the savings. (It is better than clipping coupons.) When you are getting ready for church on Sunday morning, ask God to help everything fall into place because we all know that Satan is going to make things difficult on that day. God wants to be an intimate part of our everyday life and he cannot do that unless we are communicating with him through prayer.

Finally, prayer is protection. It is the protection God promises his children throughout scripture and we cannot have it unless we ask for it. We must accept that it is our only protection from this world and all the evil within it.

2. How do we pray?

This is always an interesting thing to look at. I grew up in church and always believed that I had to pray by bowing my head and starting with "Heavenly Father". What I have experienced is quite different at times. I recall my first day in speech class at Bible College. My professor announced that we were going to open with prayer. Everyone in the room bowed their head and closed their eyes and we were all bewildered at what we heard. "Well, good morning. How are you doing today?" Everyone began to look up to see who our professor was talking too and to our amazement he was praying. At nineteen years old he was the first person to ever share the truth about the limitations we place on our prayer life. That opened a whole new thought process for me.

God cares about every detail of our lives. Please reread that. God cares about *EVERY* detail of our lives. Earlier I referred to bad hair days because it is rather important to me that I don't have them. I am a licensed cosmetologist although I no longer practice it or work in this field; it is of course important that my hair is satisfactory. When I really began to comprehend God's desire for me to be so intimate in our relationship that he cared about my bad hair days, I started praying for them to be non existent. I know some may think that it is silly but when I am getting ready and my hair doesn't work it makes me edgy and I tend to snap at whomever is around me out of my frustration. Therefore, it is a relevant thing to pray for. You see, it is preventative prayer. I understand that this is an area in my life that can cause some serious issues before church on Sunday morning and Satan knows it too. Do you think that he might use that as a tool to get everyone in a foul mood before we walk into God's house? Yes, it may be small but if it works he will use it. I also pray that God will help me to accept those days that I have to deal with it.

I hope this makes you look at things a bit differently. What about you? I know there is something small that always gets you all riled up, maybe that your husband throws his dirty clothes next to the laundry basket instead of in it? So this is what happens, you get upset and then you begin to think about everything else that he does or has done that has hurt you or made you angry with him. By the time you see him you don't want to look at him and you certainly don't want to talk to him and he doesn't even know what he has done wrong. So what can you do about this? PRAY! If you don't Satan will use it against you and before you know it you will have a huge argument and someone will say something that they will regret. Ask God to help you come up with a way to handle it that works for both of you, or for God to take away the frustration it causes you. Unfortunately he will probably not take away the laundry, but he does care about where the laundry lands because he cares about how you respond. So how do we pray for that? I believe that God wants to be not only our protector and our God but our best friend. When I pray I talk to him that way. When I am angry I don't hold that back from God because he already knows what I am feeling, so I am honest. When I am sad, I cry to him because I know he understands my pain. When I am happy, I laugh with God as I pray, I actually sometimes make jokes. That may sound a bit crazy but if he is my friend why wouldn't I talk to him as a friend? Then there are times when I cry out in my prayers. I want to show God verbally what I am feeling inwardly no matter what I am praying about.

Each individual must find their own form of communication with God. I would suggest that you try the things that I mentioned above. It may feel a bit strange at first but I promise that you will find yourself closer to God than ever before.

Now that we understand a bit more about prayer, how do we implement this into our life in regards to protecting our children from the path to abortion? Let me start by sharing that every parent should read Stormie Omartians "The Power of a Praying Parent." It is eye opening and creates for the reader a real comprehension of protecting our children through prayer. So let's look at the protection God can provide and the steps we need to take to receive it.

3. How to pray our children under the protection of God's Umbrella.

Prayer for our children is the most significant and powerful asset we have as parents or as an influence in anyone's life. We know that there is power in prayer. We know this because the Bible tells us that it so powerful when accompanied with faith it can move mountains, heal the sick, and even raise the dead. I recall several years ago a local news station reported that a research group performed a test, so to speak, on the power of prayer. The test consisted of those who were facing ailments in this particular hospital as they researched the outcome of patients who used prayer as a source of healing and those who didn't. The end result? Those who prayed to God for healing showed much greater improvement and in some cases complete recovery than those who didn't put their faith in God and his healing power. So there you have it. Research tells us what God has already promised. Prayer works!

We must remember that prayer only works when

we have the faith to believe that God will answer that prayer. *Matthew 21:22 "If you believe, you will receive whatever you ask for in prayer." Mark 11:22-24 "Have faith in God," Jesus answered. I tell you the truth, if anyone says to this mountain, 'Go, throw yourself into the sea, and does not doubt in his heart but believes that what he says will happen, it will be done for him. Therefore I tell you, whatever you ask for in prayer, believe that you have received it, and it will be yours."*.

It is the small things that lead to the larger problems and prevention and protection come when we commit to practicing prayer. When my step daughter began living with us I was concerned with school and the friends she would make being a new student at the junior high level. I remember making it a daily priority to pray that God would protect her from those who could lead her away from him. I prayed and cried out that she would find true and faithful friends that would encourage her in her walk with God. I knew that he heard me and I knew that he would honor those prayers and he did.

I pray for my teens to be protected from the temptations of sexual immorality, drugs, alcohol and all the other temptations Satan will throw at them in their most vulnerable hour. I pray for God to place in their life a true understanding of who God is and the desire to serve him. I ask God daily to instill in each of my children a great passion to reach the lost and to give them strength when they are tempted. I pray for all these things over them.

Just yesterday I prayed for my son's football team. High school football is a dangerous game and I pray for God to keep each and every boy safe. I pray for God to work in them through the football program in some way and I know that he will. I wish my son would choose a different sport and I struggled with his decision to play football because it isn't safe. As a mother I want to protect my child from any harm so the debate team sounded like a better choice to me. What I have had to accept is that God is in control of all things including what may happen to my son on the football field. The point? I have to trust in my Father and communicate to him my heart for my children. I have to ask him to bless them and watch over them. If I do not ask I will not receive.

I personally love the comparison of the umbrella. We have a wonderful friend of our family who encouraged me during some spiritual struggles about the umbrella of God. As I began to dwell on what he had said, I could only imagine this huge red umbrella and at the time mine was full of holes. I imagined my family under it in a massive storm trying to cover ourselves from the rain and wind beating down on us with this battered umbrella that was nearly no protection at all. I realized in that moment that I had a lot of hole patching to do and have been working at it ever since. My question is this, what condition is your umbrella in?

Perhaps a parent prays but does not live a godly life in the home, this creates massive holes in the umbrella of protection and that will leave their children vulnerable to getting rained on. I have watched parents go through many horrible things with their children and I listen to their mothers so broken and confused at what is going on around them. How did this happen? What did we do wrong? My heart aches for them and I pray that God will comfort them but did they put their child in God's hands through daily prayer. Did they understand the importance of the role that prayer plays in protection? I am not saying that those parents who truly pray everyday for their children will not face hardships, they may, but they will know that God has a greater purpose. Bottom line? We have to ask God to bless our children and watch over them. If we do not ask we will not receive.

Are we so busy that we cannot find time in our day to pray over our kids? Are we so busy that we cannot find time in our day to read God's word for guidance? If we find ourselves to busy we may find our children more vulnerable to temptation than we ever imagined.

Pray without ceasing. Ask God for his protection and guidance everyday. Live an honorable life before God and you will, without a doubt, live an honorable life before your children. These are the pieces to the great puzzle of parenting and all though we may sometimes share a lack of understanding, we must simply trust and understanding will come. Please remember that it is not only parents that need to adhere to these things, but each and every one of us. We all influence someone in our lives whether we are fifteen or fifty. Someone is always watching.

As we bring ourselves back to the issue of abortion, prayer will play the largest role here as well. We must pray for God to help us better comprehend what we can do in our homes and churches to promote abstinence and prevent abortion. We must pray that God will give us the ability to reach out to those who have made this choice and love them as Christ would. We must pray for the leaders of our great country to begin to seek godly wisdom in every decision they make. We must pray for one another as an encouragement that we will come together as believers, unifying our hearts for the purpose of God's will. When we do this in one accord with Christ as our guide, I truly believe we will not only experience a great revival, but we will see the tragedy of abortion change in our very lifetime.

We find ourselves at the end of this journey. My hope is that each of you has taken something of value from our time together. If I could choose just one thing for each reader to take away from this, it is that you would embrace forgiveness. It is the one gift that allows us salvation and the one gift that brings true freedom.

Chapter Ten

Gracie in October

Standing in the sanctuary on this particular Wednesday night, I felt strange, different, unlike the normal uplifting and encouraging prayer service. The lights were dim; other believers were all around me praising God in song, their hands raised as if reaching out as far as they could stretch to touch him. I, however, felt a rumble within myself. A silence within my soul was beginning to tremble as my heart began to beat so fast and so hard, I was certain those around me could hear it. I could no longer control the stream of tears that had began, as I felt uncertain of what was happening to me. The words of the song kept going through my mind, "How Great is our God." That is when it happened and I will never forget it.

As I stood at the end of the row sobbing, I heard

a little girl say excitedly, "Mommy! Mommy!" I set my attention on the aisle that leads to the front of the sanctuary, and there, running to me was a beautiful little girl with curly brown hair and big brown eyes. There was a teddy bear tucked under her arm and she wore the biggest smile I have ever seen. She was looking right at me, calling to me, and she knew exactly who I was. No one else seemed to see her or notice what was happening, but I did. I knew she was my Gracie.

It was in the month of October that this took place, which was somewhat ironic because it was the hardest month of the year for me. It was this month that Gracie would have been born. That vision, dream, or moment that I experienced, I could only see her as a toddler but in actuality, she would have been 10 years old. Even though she never made it all the way to my seat in that Wednesday night prayer service, I knew that God was working in a miraculous way. I had known for some time that God was knocking at my hearts door and I wanted so badly to give in completely but I could not totally surrender. I now see that I had never truly forgiven myself for the choice that I had made in March of 1995. God knew that my self-sacrifice, self-discipline, and desire to serve him would not be enough without a most important ingredient; self-forgiveness. I did not know where to begin on the road to forgiving myself but I knew that it was necessary if I had any intentions of serving God in any other capacity.

I walked out of the church, rounded up my children and headed home; my entire thought process focused on the vision that God had so graciously blessed me with. I could think of nothing else. Thoughts of my Gracie consumed me and left me in a near state of hypnosis. The questions pondered one after the other; "would she have looked like that? What would she love doing the most? Would she have enjoyed cooking with me? What would it have been like to hold her?" All of these questions and thoughts surrounded me as if a pack of wolves were surrounding its prey. As I continued to wander off into the "what if" of my life, I realized that my children were now screaming "MOM!" in hopes of gaining my undivided attention.

As I listened to them, excited about the youth services, I found that I could see Gracie in each of them. Through a smile, through the sound of their laughter, through the touch of their love. Then, it hit like a brick...how could I have done it? I killed her; she would be here right now, right here, in this car but I killed her! I can never forgive myself for that! How can I ever forgive myself for that?

The atmosphere became quiet as if my children knew of the choice I had once made. I felt they could see what was going on in my mind like watching a movie and my darkest secrets were unfolding before them. They could never know of this choice, and if they did, could they ever understand or forgive me?

It seemed somewhat lonely after getting everyone off to bed with my husband away on business. I took a seat in front of the office computer and began to look up sights on abortion, I had never seen an abortion in its entirety but for some reason I was drawn to the true understanding of 'choice'. There it was, in my face, and God wanted me to see it! Who better to know what I needed than the one that created me, right? He fashioned me to comprehend life from a pictorial point of communication. This is when the realization of my choice hit me in such a way that in order to find a deserving reason to live, I would have to forgive myself.

The pictures of aborted babies from facilities across the country were seared into my mind. Some of these babies were almost full term and lay helpless and defeated. I began to feel nauseous which only became worse with each picture. These were not fetuses, they were not blobs of tissue, they were babies! As I stumbled through my tears, which had now turned to weeping, I remember saying one thing aloud; "there's little arms and feet." My mind took over like a flood of water rushing back to almost eighteen years ago as the words rang repeatedly in my ears; "now it's taken arms, my little legs and feet." For the first time in ten years I finally accepted it, I finally became responsible for it, I fully comprehended my choice...***my choice***. For me, this was the first step in moving toward self-forgiveness. It was my choice to be sexually immoral, it was my choice to take the chance of pregnancy and it was my choice to walk through the doors of that abortion clinic.

The words that rang so loud to me may seem familiar to you as you have made your way through this journey with me. You may be asking yourself where you heard that before. It was in a poem that I once wrote for a high school term paper, "Mommy Why?" It was at that time, my greatest work of poetry. Yes, that was my experience, my choice, my story. I never would have dreamed that it would be the one piece that would forever remind me of my own hypocrisy. Never did I imagine it too would be the one work that would throw my sins back in my face. Never, did I believe that it would be the one poetic creation that would one day bring me back to a real place of humility and forgiveness.

As the rain poured onto the roof of our old farmhouse, it was time, and God was calling. Reading that poem again, I contemplated the path I had taken in this life and I reached for a God who promised to forgive me. I cried out to a Father who wants my future and forgets my past. In a fetal position, my floor became a temporary place of residence as my Heavenly Father comforted me and welcomed me with open arms into his own. I wept as never before for the loss of my baby. After hours of letting go of the pain and suffering of my abortion, I found a new freedom, a new joy. For the first time in my life, I embraced and had full clarity of the meaning of a peace that passes all understanding.

Gracie May would have been born in October of 1995. She would be 11 Years old today as I write of her. It was in October of 2005 that I saw a vision or glimpse of Gracie. It was also in October of 2005 that my life changed and forgiveness, accompanied by a future, became a reality. I named my baby Gracie May because it reminds me of God's Amazing Grace and how I would be lost without it, for it was in October that I truly found it. For my Gracie, I love you my child, whom I did not save, but who saved me...in October.

Frequently Asked Questions and Suggestions on Abortion Prevention

Q. *What is the most important thing that I can do as a parent, grandparent, family member or friend to protect my loved ones from making this devastating choice?*

S. Obviously you are already aware that they may make a mistake here. If you are living your life honorably before God, you are living honorably before them as well. This means you have already given them a strong foundation and a great example to follow. ***The most important thing you can do is pray!*** You must love them as you share your concerns with them. Pray first for God to give you compassion and understanding. Second, pray that God will prepare them to receive what you have to say in a positive way and that he will give you the correct timing and words to do it with. ***Talk to***

them not at them about what you are concerned with. DO not be angry or frustrated because they will sense it and they will immediately turn you off. Share real stories with them, they understand best through stories. Tell them yours if you have one that is relevant to the situation. They need to know you are not perfect.

Q. *What can I do to help someone who has decided to have an abortion?*

S. First, ask the Lord for guidance in what to say. Second, hug them and tell them that you love them. Create a safe environment for them so they feel that they can open up and talk to you about it. **You will never be able to help them see the reality of abortion if you do not allow them to feel safe!** They must feel that you are trustworthy, you will not condemn them and you will be there. You must allow them to share without pressure. Only then will you be able to encourage them and share stories like mine so they may understand the truth of the decision they face. Remember, they feel cornered and they are looking for someone to rescue them. They feel alone and they need to know someone is there. It is a gift from God to have an opportunity such as this so please allow God to lead the conversation and you may very well be used by God to save a precious life.

Q. *What can I say to my child if I feel that they are becoming involved in sexual activity to avoid ever being faced with this choice?*

S. One of the best conversations I have had with my teenage step daughter was concerning the subject of sex. Instead of first drowning her in scripture, I broke the ice by utilizing the situation in her own life. She struggles with fact that she has two families that are 1000 miles apart. She has a step brother and several half sisters and a half brother. I know this is frustrating for her and she does not want this for her own life. I used this situation to begin the conversation with something that she would relate to and understand. As she began to open up I was *then* able to utilize scripture as a tool **because she was listening.** She felt safe talking to me in that moment and she trusted what I said. We always push abstinence first and foremost but you must continue into the 'what if' that doesn't work. Through this conversation I created a scenario of possibility that she one day makes a decision and finds herself with an unplanned pregnancy. I asked her what she would do. It was then that I shared with her my past choice and the effect it had on me throughout my life.

Play out a possible circumstance. Ask them if they would feel comfortable enough to tell you if they were ever in that situation. Ask them how they would want you to react and what they would want you to say. This will help you prepare for any situation that you may face with them, not just pregnancy or abortion. Assure them that you will be disappointed and hurt but you won't love them any less and you will be there to help them through it. Most importantly, make sure they understand that they are more important to you then what others may think in any type of circumstances.

Q. *If I want to talk to my child about abortion, how do I even begin?*

S. For some this is very uncomfortable but it is crucial for your children to understand that you are open to the topic. They hear it on TV, the radio, and see it plastered on billboards. They know it is real and they know it is available to them, so don't be afraid to talk about it, or they may never know the other side of it until it is too late. It is your day in court, so to speak, so don't be afraid to do this! You have to grasp that the world has had their time to invade your child's mind and they aren't done yet. It is your duty to clear up the confusion or lack of interpretation they have of abortion. That means something you are expected or required to do by moral or legal obligation; it is your duty as a parent.

Begin with me. Tell them that you read a book where a young woman shared her story of a life of bad choices. Don't hold back, I don't mind. If you can use my life story to protect your children from abortion, **PLEASE DO SO!** When you begin sharing this, it will remove them from the center of the conversation and they will not feel threatened. Please accept that if they have had thoughts of sex or have done anything they feel is over the line, what you say could be crucial to shutting an open line of communication. *By removing them completely, they can engage and share their thoughts and feelings.* They may bring up a friend that has faced this, someone they know right now that might be contemplating it. This is a **HUGE opportunity** for you. By the questions they ask and responses they give you during the conversation, you will begin to have clarity of how they view and feel about this issue. Remember, the best way to hear them is to listen. *THIS NEEDS YOUR UNDIVIDED ATTENTION!* Turn off the cell phone, the house phone, the TV, and don't worry about dinner. Know that there is nothing else in that room but your child. If you don't focus on them completely, they will not feel important and they will not feel comfortable talking with you about this or any other issue in the future!

Q. *Should I allow my child to view some of the information on the web?*

S. This is of course a decision you have to make but be very careful. The Silent Scream is a video that does not show graphic detail but will give them an idea of what happens to the baby during an abortion. There are other videos and information out there but the graphic pictures may need to wait until it is absolutely necessary. (When you are sure they have become sexually active, they know someone considering abortion, or you are confident that they are mature enough to handle it.) My suggestion here is that you allow them to look at a couple of websites that have been set up just for teens and college aged girls. Please view them yourself before you give your permission but these sites share real stories, real circumstances and the consequences of choices. It will reach them because the girls they are reading about are girls just like them.

www.teenbreaks.com www.standupgirl.com

If you are sharing my story and they are asking questions, that is a perfect time to say, hey, here's a couple of websites you can go to. Do you want to look at them together? If they say no, don't get upset. If you have already looked the sites over and approved, let them search for themselves. Sometimes, it is best to let God do his work without you.

Q. *I want to talk to my child but it never seems to work, what can I do?*

S. In some cases it is very difficult to communicate with our children so I will share a trick that I have used with my teenager. (You can use this for any issue but best if used on a daily basis.)

Get a journal. Write a letter to your child explaining to them how much you love them and want to talk to them. Tell them that you understand that it is hard. Maybe you want them to know that it was hard for you to talk to your parents too. Share with them that this journal is just for the two of you and no one else will ever see it. Set rules and stick by them. Your child has to drop it in your special place by 9:00 PM and you have to have it returned by 10:00 AM or whatever works for both of you. Have them write in it at night and put it in the secret special place you have both agreed on before they go to bed. You will pick it up in the morning, write back and place it back for them to retrieve by the next day. They enjoy the fact this is something special between the two of you. It is also intriguing due to the fact that it is a secret place, a safe place, a mysterious form of communication. You will find that they will want to know what you have to say and will open up about many things over time. **PLEASE BE SURE** that you always, always, always return the book by the time agreed upon. If they go to get it and it isn't there you will find they are more disappointed than expected and they will feel as if it wasn't important enough for you to follow the rules. ***THIS IS VITAL!***

This form of communication removes facial expression, body language, and inflections of the voice; therefore, there is no condemnation. (Unless you write it out, so don't!) Always start with positives about them, their life, their friends and what you are proud of that they do or have done. Pick something they did that day that made you smile or laugh or proud. Add the questions you have or issues you want to address in the center of the letter in a loving way. You don't have to beat around the bush but don't be sarcastic or assuming. End with positive reinforcement as you started. If they begin feeling good and they end feeling good, suddenly the middle isn't so hard to swallow.

Please know that I am in no way trying to tell anyone how to raise their children. I am simply giving you suggestions that will assist you in learning how your child thinks and feels about this and other important issues. These are things that have worked for me with my children and I believe would have made a huge difference in my life and my choices. I hope they may help you as well. From my own experience and the experiences of the women that have shared their stories with me, all of this would have made a devastating choice, not so devastating.

Frequently Asked Questions and Suggestions on Post Abortion Situations

Q. *What do I do when someone I know has had an abortion and I can see they need help?*

S. You must first understand that a woman who has already made this choice has condemned herself to an eternity in hell. She is the worst of sinners, she is the unforgivable one. There is no sin greater in her mind. ***She will be sensitive, extremely sensitive.*** Prayer is going to play a major role (more so than in the prevention suggestions) because every look, sound, and movement will be read as possible judgment. You may say or do something that is meant one way but taken another. Not because you are doing anything wrong (if you are letting God lead you), but because

Satan is in their ear telling them you are judging them. He doesn't want them to see that God has provided a way out. If they do, Satan will no longer have a hold on them and believe me, abortion is his favorite toy when it comes to women.

Pray for timing, pray for hearts to be receptive and for God to lead you when you speak. Pray for guidance in what to say when you do communicate and when to simply love and listen. To sum it all up, **you must create a safe place for them. It is the most important factor in reaching any woman, no matter what the issue.**

Q. *I found out that my child had an abortion, I'm angry and hurt, what do I do?*

S. At this point, it is already done. They cannot take back their choice, they cannot redo that day, so going backward will help no one. Yelling at them, ignoring them, cutting off you're affection from them will only intensify their self inflicted condemnation. There is nothing you can say or do that they haven't already thought about themselves. In many cases, suicidal thoughts are frequent and unfortunately in some cases, tragic realities.

What they need to know is that they not only have a loving Father and Savior who wants to forgive them but they have loving parents who want to do the same. Your disappointment is expected but your judgment will only cause them to become more distant. I guarantee that if you handle this in the right manner, you will not only be able to grieve and heal together, you will build a bond that will forever be unbroken.

Love them as Christ has loved you and forgiven you for all the things that you have done. Let them know that you will be there to help them get through this but do it at their pace. Don't pressure them into doing anything that will make them feel uncomfortable. When they need to cry, have your shoulder ready and cry with them. When they need to talk, just listen. This will not be an easy journey but it will be a journey that can change your entire relationship with them. It is a journey worth taking because as you become closer, you can steer them away form making more mistakes. Many women feel as if they have nothing left because they are undeserving of real love, the love of a Savior. This causes them to fall into a downward spiral of bad choices. Protect them from that. Try to understand their pain. You may never understand their choice, but you can understand their pain if you watch closely enough.

Q. *I found out someone close to me had an abortion and I can't stand to look at them, how do I get past this?*

S. This happens often when we feel that someone we care for has done something we can't comprehend or don't approve of. Abortion is ugly just to hear it but to know how close to home it hits is sometimes more ugly than we can handle. My suggestion is that we must try to accept that sin is sin. God does not put limits on what sin is greater than another, we do that. Paul, the writer of a large portion of the New Testament, willingly murdered hundreds of believers. David took the life of a man who was incredibly loyal to him just to cover his own sin. God loved these men and used them in a mighty way. Try to grasp that God is bigger than we are and his love is deeper than we can fathom. Ask him to give you peace. Ask him to fill your heart with love and compassion for that person. Ask him to allow you to see your own faults rather than focusing on someone else's.

Final Thoughts

I used to think these women were the worst of humans. I believed there was no redemption for them before my own choice to abort. Because of my arrogance of believing I was better than them, I myself have been humbled in more ways than one. I no longer make a habit of judging others; I now make a habit of loving them. If any good is to come from my choice it is that I now understand that God's love is not conditioned. It is unfailing, bigger than the universe and that He wants our future, not our past. God can take any circumstance, ugly and hideous, and make it beautiful. That is why he is perfect and we are not. If you seek him and ask him for these things, with a genuine heart, he will open your eyes and you will begin to see life more clear than you ever have before.

The Bible tells us that God chose us before creation. He knew all that we would be and every decision that we would make and he still chose us. Philippians 1:6 "being confident of this, that he who began a good work in you will carry it out to completion until the day of Christ Jesus." He began a good work in us, all of us. It is God that will complete that work if we allow him to do so; no matter what we have done in our past.

Information and Tools on

Abstinence and Abortion Prevention

This section could be of great importance to every parent, guardian, minister, teacher or anyone in a position of influence. It is also a resource for those young men and women looking for answers to a real life crisis. The information provided here is for use at your discretion. These tools can help you talk to your children or others about abstinence and abortion.

Statistical Information for this project was based on results obtained by the following.

The Guttmacher Institue
www.guttmacher.com
Abortion Facts Organization
www.abortionfacts.com

Other sources were also researched but results were equal to those as listed above.

Parents: *Please pray and ask God for guidance as you begin this journey.*

The following sites listed under 'Teens' need be to be approved by an adult prior to using them. In many cases, teens will not talk to you about the issues listed in the following websites so be sure to check them out thoroughly. There are some that have no faith-based connection but seem to promote the choice of life. *I have not been able to check every site in its entirety and cannot vouch for its complete content.*

Again, I strongly urge each parent, guardian, pastor, or other to research each of the sites I have listed. **Do not allow your child, youth group or family members, who may be facing these issues to view these sites until you have approved them.** Use these resources to find books, counseling services or forums to help you in your quest to share the truth of sexuality with our world.

www.youthdevelopment.suite101.com
This site gives great ideas for parent and teen activities.

www.physiciansforlife.com
This site is full of information, suggestions and statistics. I have researched portions of this site and found that some of the information is very good. I would suggest parents look through all the information and see what the government is doing when it comes to abstinence, pregnancy and abortion. It is also important to understand the medical ramifications of what our young people are facing today.

www.choosingthebest.org
This is a site you need to check out. I have only researched a portion of its content but I encourage you to go to the curriculum page and watch the sample video. Even after being married for several years it was intriguing to listen to what these individuals had to say. It is a site dedicated to abstinence and provides resources for parents, teachers and others. I found no faith based tie to this site, therefore some of the information they provide you may not agree with.

www.afterabortion.org

This site is run by an organization called Elliot Institute. It is full of information on abortion. It is also provides up-to-date accounts of what is happening with our government in regard to abortion, parental rights, statistics, embryo development, and how we can help those who have already made this choice.

www.abortionfacts.com

When entering this site you can chose 'pro-life' or pro-choice' it will then take you to several links including how and why the courts legalized abortion in the Roe VS. Wade controversy.

http://blog.cleveland.com/lifestyles/2008/ 06/cleveland_churches_take_open_a.html

This is a link to a great article on how one church is taking action and how it's working.

www.focusonthefamily.com

This site is wonderful for parents. The format is not set up, in my opinion, to draw the younger generation but for those of you in a position of influence for that generation; it is worth your time. Not only does it give information on many of the topics of today including homosexuality, abstinence, gambling and more, it also has forums that can assist you as well. This is a great resource site.

www.bethany.org

If as a parent you are facing the unplanned pregnancy of a child, please go the 'my daughter is pregnant link". Even if this pregnancy affects your son, please look at this section. It provides guidance and resources for you to find help.

Teens: *Please be sure to get parents permission before viewing these sites.*

You can email me directly and I will try to help you in any way that I can. Please know that you will not be judged. The email address is **change.lifeinterrupted@gmail.com**

www.teenbreaks.com

This site deals with today's issues. From unplanned pregnancy, depression, drug and alcohol abuse, suicide, rape, incest, abusive relationships, eating disorders, self-cutting and more. Nearly any issue is addressed in this site. These are stories of real teens facing real world problems. A great site for parents to view and approve.

www.standupgirl.com

A site designed for girls who have found themselves in an unwanted pregnancy. This site gives great information, brings truth of the situation upfront and center, and provides a safe environment.

www.christianitytoday.com

This is full of real life stories facing every issue in today's world. It tells the truth uncut and shares stories of others who have walked through them and how your faith can be your greatest tool.

www.inspiringabstinence.com

This site has pages for parents, teens, and others accompanied by statistics which can be an eye opening experience. It also has resources available that could be very useful in effectively communicating for all age groups.

www.OptionLine.org

Site designed to help you make the best decision if you find yourself pregnant or facing an STD. Options and medical facts on these options are provided for you. *PARENTS, PLEASE CHECK AND APPROVE THIS SITE!*

www.bethany.org

If you find yourself or a friend in an unplanned pregnancy, you can go to this site, click on the 'how do I tell them I'm pregnant link' and it will give you great advice and the encouragement you need to take this first step.

www.abortionpain.com

If you are facing abortion choices, go to this link, click on choices, click on abortion. It will share the truth of this choice.

If you do not have internet access, there are local pregnancy centers that you can contact by phone. The National Hotline is *1-800-848-LOVE (5683)* they can direct you to a local agency if needed.

Post-Abortion: *For those who have had an abortion and don't know where to turn.*

www.abortionpain.com

Many of your questions can be answered along with a guide to beginning the healing process.

www.afterabortion.org

This is a site that will give you tools and resources to help you understand that you are not alone and how to begin your journey on the path to healing.

www.silentnomoreawareness.org

This will give you insight to healing, where to begin, what you will face along the way and where you can find the help you need. It also shares the truth about what type of help you seek.

Check your local churches. There are some who offer abortion recovery classes. I know it is hard to attend or inquire about this but please believe me when I say that it can change your life. It was because of this program being offered at my church that this book was even written. Local pregnancy crisis centers many times offer this as well.

If you have questions or would like more information feel free to email me at change.lifeinterrupted@gmail.com